TO HORSE! TO HORSE!

BY
TERRY WOGAN
&
TONY FAIRBAIRN

FOREWORD BY SIR IAN TRETHOWAN

ILLUSTRATIONS BY JOHN IRELAND

Willow Books
Collins
St James's Place, London
1982

Willow Books
William Collins & Co Ltd
London Glasgow Sydney Auckland
Toronto Johannesburg

Wogan, Terry and Fairbairn, Tony
To horse! To horse!
1. Horse-racing—Anecdotes, facetiae, satire, etc.
I. Title   II. Fairbairn, Tony
798.4   SF334

ISBN 0–00–218085–5

First published 1982
Copyright © Terry Wogan and Tony Fairbairn 1982

Made by Lennard Books
The Old School
Wheathampstead, Herts AL4 8AN

Editor Michael Leitch
Designed by David Pocknell's Company Ltd
Production Reynolds Clark Associates Ltd
Printed and bound in Spain by
TONSA, San Sebastian
Dep. Legal: S.S. 391 – 1982

CONTENTS

FOREWORD BY
SIR IAN TRETHOWAN

When, more than a dozen years ago, I became the Managing Director of BBC Radio, two things soon happened. Through my insistence, we started the morning Racing Bulletin; without any intervention from me at all, we acquired a young (or youngish) Irish bank clerk as a disc jockey. In due course, the two came together, and ever since Terry Wogan has been taking the mickey out of racing, and out of me since I became Director-General. Racing men who may wince at some of Terry's outrageous quips at least knew he was being just as irreverent about his boss – and all of us can seek consolation in backing Wogan's Winner (but not too heavily!).

I have always felt Terry's approach to racing has one particular advantage: he reminds us that behind this many-million-pound industry there are millions of people for whom it is just entertainment, a bit of fun. This book sets out to lace the fun with facts. All of us who love racing will remember the first time we set foot on the racecourse. We will remember the sense of awe and bewilderment. What is a 'handicap'? What is a 'forecast'? What of the 'draw'? And the 'going'? Why are some races longer than others? Our questions were endless.

We all had to begin somewhere, and a book like this, drawing on Terry's inimitable humour and the deep knowledge of Tony Fairbairn and the Racing Team, provides a painless, amusing but useful place for beginners to start learning about racing – and for old hands to brush up on the facts, and pick up some good racing jokes.

INTRODUCTION

'To horse! To horse!' That is the cry, the merry view-halloo that jerks the unsuspecting listener from his Radio 2-induced slumber at 8.32 every weekday morning. Well, more or less. It can also be 'Clamber Oop De Beesties!', a hearty Flemish blandishment, carrying roughly the same equine message. I say 'roughly', because I'm not entirely sure if it doesn't have another, more unsavoury connotation, which my Belgian friends are keeping from me. I occasionally receive enigmatic postcards from Europe carrying the piquant inquiry: 'Do you have any idea what that disgusting phrase means?'

No! And I don't want to know. It is enough that the jolly Belgian bellow has the tang of the tack-room about it. It seems to steam, like a Cheltenham winner. Or a Cheltenham punter, come to that . . . .

Given, as we are, to the polyglot expression, the listener and I often lapse into Gallic braggadocio: 'Au Cheval!' I intone, or 'Aux Chevaux!', which unaccountably causes many impressionable punters to rush off to the barber's instead of their local meeting. The listener has offered many suggestions to relieve the tedium, many of them involving one-way tickets to some far-flung hell-hole or other. These I ignore as unworthy, and welcome instead such *phrases utiles* as 'Au Chapeau!' or, if the weather is inclement, 'Au Château!' . . . *you're* confused?

TERRY WOGAN

THE SPORTING LIFE
OR
MY TIMES IN RACING

TO HORSE! TO HORSE!

My father was a keen punter but, through a maze of each-way doubles and trebles, never seemed to expend more than five bob. In the manner and tradition of all great British and Irish off-shore punters, he did not actually attend race meetings. It was one of my great pleasures in his declining years to take him to the great British racecourses, Windsor, Newbury and Ascot, where, of course, he was completely at sea. Turf accountants' offices he understood, but the hurly-burly of the racecourse itself, with its shouted odds, the bustling and the heckling of the bookies, the betting on numbers instead of names on the Tote, all combined to confuse him utterly. I *think* he enjoyed himself, but whether it was an act designed to keep a well-meaning son happy, I'll never know.

I think my father, like myself, enjoyed the people more than the horses. On these occasions, with a couple of glasses of the right stuff inside him, he became known as 'The Kissing Bandit'. Not much of a one for the torrid embrace in his sober moments, he was a terror with the champagne lapping up against his back teeth. He kissed everyone. Those who were lucky enough to escape on the basis of gender or foreign aspect, he engaged in airy banter or deep conversation. I mind well the occasion at Windsor where he trapped an unwary Chinese gentleman and questioned him closely on the Communist Government, and, specifically, Mao. Since the gentleman was a member

of the Hong Kong Jockey Club, had never been to mainland China in his life, and my father insisted on pronouncing Mao as 'Mayo', you hardly need me to describe how confused the conversation became. I didn't intervene, for fear of The Kissing Bandit turning his attentions on some unsuspecting dowager. . . .

Since he didn't deign to attend himself, my father saw no need to introduce me in my formative years to the arcane pleasures of the Irish race-tracks. I have a vague recollection of being taken by bus to

the Irish Grand National at Fairyhouse, when scarcely out of knee-breeches, by my kindly Uncle Eddie. Why he saw fit to lumber himself with a mewling, and if I remember correctly, puking infant (long bus journeys always upset my delicate stomach), I do not understand. He was rewarded for his kindliness and endurance however, because I distinctly remember him backing the winner. The extraordinary thing is, I can also distinctly remember the winner's name: Alberoni. Nothing else. I don't have the slightest glimmer about the day, the journey or the crowds, just the name of a winning horse. And don't ask how long ago that was. It's one side of the thing I'd *rather* not remember. . . .

Suffice to say, it was a considerable number of years before I chanced my delicate stomach and pocket-book at another race-meeting. I must have been all of twenty summers, when, pursuant to my then policy of becoming the Burlington Bertie of Grafton Street, and

Lothario-in-Chief of the Dublin Coffee Bar Set, I took a couple of gels along in my Morris Minor, with the broken front passenger seat, to the Mecca of Dublin Racing Society, the Phoenix Park. I must be getting older than even *you* suspect, because I remember little about *that* meeting, either. Even the gels' faces are a hazy memory, and I certainly cannot remember any horses' names, so we can't have backed any winners (a tradition which I carry on proudly to this very day). It was sunny though, and fun, and *smart*. People were dressed in their best, the men dressing for the benefit and approval of the women, and the women dressing for the benefit and approval of other women. The one thing that sticks in my memory about Phoenix Park is that you never knew who won any race until it was announced over the public address system. The finishing post was out of sight of the enclosures and most of the stands. The horses would belt hell-for-leather round the course, then past the corner of the main stand, where they were seen no more; a great cheer would greet the unseen winner, and everybody held on grimly to their tickets until the announcement was made. Some may think it peculiarly Irish to have a winning-post that none of the paying customers could see, but it certainly added *frisson*. Who cared, anyway? We were only there for the 'crack'.

For reasons that escape me, I subsequently attended race-meetings at Navan (it rained), and Leopardstown just outside Dublin. Actually, the present Lady Wogan and I attended Leopardstown quite a lot in our heady courting days. It was a pleasant way to spend a summer evening: you invariably met friends or made new ones, shared drinks and tips at the bar, rarely saw a race, and had only the occasional punt, for the sake of appearances.

The Irish have a great reputation as racegoers. 'Racing-mad' is how I've heard my fellow countrymen described. It's a reputation based on tales of bets and coups from Galway to Epsom, from Ascot to Limerick Junction.

Certainly the Irish are proud of their horses, and proud of their own knowledge of those horses – but 'racing-mad'? No. It's the 'crack': the cocking of the snook at the racing authorities, the besting of the bookies; but most of all, the talking and the singing, the laughing and the drinking – never mind the winning or the losing, as long as the 'crack' is good, the job is right.

TERRY WOGAN
WOGAN'S WINNER

TO HORSE! TO HORSE!

I'll tell you a tale of the Beeb lads,
Where they play all the latest hits,
And the harsh rending sound
You can hear from the ground
Is the DG performing the splits.

Ah! But what is that terrible smell,
lads?
From that shed almost hidden from
view,
Hang your heads in disgrace
For this is the place
Where they melt Wogan's Winners for
glue!
Anon.

Yes, friends, just one more hurtful barb in the seemingly endless flow of contumely and insult which I receive every morning from faithful listeners to my Radio 2 Breakfast Show. Just one of the many to cast doubt on my abilities as a Tipster, a Man Steeped in the Lore of the Turf, a Son of the Ould Sod . . . .

Well now, let me boldly say straight away that if what I don't know about horses was placed end to end, it would encircle Cyril Smith, who knows even less. You're looking at a man who can't tell a fetlock from a forelock, a Hock from a Moselle.

Oh, I know I dole out the Racing Information, and confidently tip 'Wogan's Winner' every morning, but anybody who knows one end of a horse from another sees through my little pantomime, and does not confuse my gabbling with equine

16

knowledge. Quite the reverse, if the dog's abuse I take from cab-drivers, merry matrons and refuse disposal operatives is anything to go by:

'Call yourself a tipster, Terry? You couldn't tip *Rubbish*! Har! Har!' Or:

'Ere, Ter, how much are the bookies payin' you, then?'

Ground opens up and swallows our hero, suffused with embarrassment . . . .

Look here, the Racing Information Bulletin was being broadcast every morning on Radio 2 long before I left my permanent pensionable position in banking for the tinsel glamour and brittle gaiety of showbiz. It's not my fault that some eejit had the bright idea that I should end each bulletin with a suggestion as to where the put-upon punter should stick the last of the Children's Allowance. The Racing News, *and* the tip, come from that admirable, if slightly down-at-heel body of men, the Racing Information Bureau. This world-weary band of mug-punters are Racing's Publicity and PR Men – though what sort of PR Wogan's Winner provides for racing one can only surmise!

Anyway, in they troop to my little studio, in the sleazy back alleys of the BBC, racing hats pulled down over their low foreheads, a copy of the *Sporting Life* sticking out of the pockets of their shredded plastic macs, carrying with them all the tittle-tattle of the stable-yard, as well as some of its less-pleasing odours.

'There you are, guvnor, hope that it's to your satisfaction,' they whine ingratiatingly, handing me a crumpled ill-written sheet. 'What about Wogan's Winner yesterday?' I snarl. 'Carried off by a loose 'orse, guv, jockey 'ad to jump for 'is life!' comes the snivelling, apologetic excuse. I cuff the advisor heavily about the head, and let him have a few stinging lashes of my riding-crop about his fetlocks and hams. The unfortunate fellow cringes in a corner while I read the racing information to an eager listening public that includes HM Queen Elizabeth The Queen Mother, Humphrey Cottrill, and various owners, whose screams of 'Why me? Why me?' can be heard for miles if I so much as mention their old nags.

For the foul calumny persists that The Winner is a Loser, that having their noble steed selected by our hero is tantamount to The Kiss of Death. And rightly so.

If it were otherwise, I would never have been exonerated, without a stain on my wholesome character, by The Churches' Council on Gambling. While they jumped all over Newsboy, Goodfellow and O'Sullevan in cleated boots, they felt that *my* advice constituted a positive discouragement to prospective punters.

It's not all Hell on Hooves, though. The occasional winner does come through, despite everything. When it does, I brazenly take all the credit. This has not escaped the eagle ear of the listener:

Dear Racing Advisor,
The time has now come when you must give Terry a belt in the earole everytime it wins. Everytime it loses he really puts you through it, but when it wins, he wants all the praise. If this does not work, try feeding him bit by bit to Jimmy Young.
Yours faithfully,
Stanley Gerrard

TONY FAIRBAIRN

WOGAN'S WINNER?
WOGAN'S NOTHING!

TO HORSE! TO HORSE!

Talk about ingratitude! 'Down at heel', 'ingratiating', 'snivelling', 'world-weary mug-punters'. What contemptuous unfeeling defamation. What hurtful calumny. What disparaging nasturtiums to cast upon the wholly conscientious, selfless and totally dedicated team of advisers who spurn the favours of their wives, eschew the warmth and comfort of their firesides, and lock themselves away from the merry laughter of their children as they devote their lives to the provision of a daily gift-horse for this immigrant disc-jockey. But this blustering buffoon looks it in the mouth, and rewards with arrogant taunts their hours of careful research, the midnight study and the painstaking analysis of races past – not to mention their capital investment in the gleaming steel of Sheffield's finest pins.

Occasionally, of course, the hours spent lying in a muddy Newmarket ditch to await the secret dawn gallop of a Derby favourite, the pints of old and mild poured into Lambourn stable lads, and the employment of Senior Wranglers in Mathematics to calculate the weight, time and distance equation in relation to windspeeds and variable rainfall are to no avail. Some totally unforeseen circumstance arises to upset the confident predictions upon which the nation depends to pay its gas bills. The unpredictable can deal a cruel blow, and Wogan's Winners, it must be admitted, do, from time to time, get beaten despite the efforts of yours truly and the rest of the team – Laurie Brannan, Paul Mathieu and John Santer.

It is then that the fiery Irish temper is at its most fearsome. Gone is the equable humour, the cheery banter which characterizes Radio 2 as its listeners gulp their Wheatybangs or fillet a kipper prior to the start of another day in search of another dollar.

The Wogan is a hard taskmaster. It is understandable that he should be unforgiving of error, but unforgiveable that he should be so lacking in understanding as to denigrate his devoted equine intelligence service on those occasions when success was snatched from their grasp by the temporary incapacity of a jockey with haemorrhoids, a starter with a hangover or a horse with constipation. It is, after all, only these and other such incalculable strokes of fate which lie behind that rare national disaster, a Wogan's Loser.

In his wrath this tipster of the turntable gives not so much as a passing thought to the trophies displayed so proudly on his baby grand, chrome and plastic, Japanese-imported, amaze-your-friends, no-skill-required, electric organ, the musical microchip monster which buckles under their weight at Wogan Towers. The crystal and silver honours bestowed on him for broadcasting the advice of others mean nothing to him on those isolated days when their skills and talents have been thwarted by the delayed recovery of an over-indulgent rider. Forgotten are the five consecutive seasons when Wogan's Winner actually showed a consistent profit, including the memorable

summer when the daily wager showed a bigger credit balance than that of the winner of the *Sporting Life's* Naps Table! Significantly, perhaps, most of these successes of yesteryear were achieved before the jockey population was scourged with a plague of piles.

Nevertheless the two most recent jumping seasons have seen Wogan walk off with the Haig Trophy awarded to the most successful tipster in the series of 42 races – one on each hurdles course in the country – sponsored by the whisky firm. Mind you, on such occasions the credit goes not to the snivelling, cringing advisers whose dedicated application made it all possible but to this seedy, unshaven Irishman sitting in front of a microphone, terrorizing the turf-accountants with his daily bookie-busting certainty.

Winners are unquestionably Wogan's, losers the responsibility of the advisers. After all, was it not himself who after three consecutive winners acknowledged the presence of his racing adviser with an imperious 'Who is the star of this show?' But the listeners are more perceptive than he thinks, and it was not only the adviser's advisory talents which led lovelorn Valerie – a perspicacious London lass – to pen the following:

That sexy voice with sonorous tones
Assails my ears each day:
The manly frame it conjures up could
*   have its wicked way*
With me at anytime, she said,
Oh dear, my face is getting red!
Oh were I older and a great deal
*   wiser,*
But I'm madly in love with your
*   Racing Adviser!!!*

TO HORSE! TO HORSE!

Saturday is a day off for Wogan, but not, of course, for racing which has its busiest day of the week. So the Racing Bulletin is produced as usual and read by the Radio 2 Duty Announcer.

Several years ago the lovely Sarah Kennedy was faced with this task for the first time. As is the normal practice, she was given the basic script twenty minutes or so before going on the air to familiarize herself with the pronunciation of some of the more eccentric names. The final updated version of the script would be delivered just a few minutes before the broadcast.

The script that day included the observation that 'Mai Pussy, triumphant at Doncaster earlier this week, is looking for further success this afternoon.' Read by James Alexander-Gordon, no-one would give the sentence a second thought, but from the charming Miss Kennedy?

Back in the Sportsroom I was taking telephone calls from the various Clerks of Course reporting the latest going conditions, when in walked Brian Johnston to contribute a cricket report to *Sport on Four*. Such a senior broadcaster was just the man to advise on the delicate problem I was facing.

'Brian,' I said, showing him the script. 'What do you think about this line, bearing in mind that it is to be read by the delectable Sarah Kennedy? Perhaps I should change it?'

'Change it,' bellowed Brian. 'Good Heavens no! I want to record it!'

Returning to the studio with the final version of the script, I still had misgivings, and sympathy for Sarah made me ask her if she had noticed any particular problem.

'Noticed it,' she snorted. 'Of course I've noticed it, and no way am I going to say it!'

But before I had a chance to amend the script Sarah came up with her own solution. 'Look,' she said, 'Mai is spelt MAI so rather than pronounce it "My" I propose saying "May", if that's OK with you.' I mumbled agreement, and that's how it was broadcast. Sadly though, Brian never switched on the recorder.

TONY FAIRBAIRN
THE RACEGOER

TO HORSE! TO HORSE!

Although more than ninety per cent of all betting on horseracing takes place away from the racecourse, it is upon the little army of racegoers that the whole of racing is ultimately dependent. They are the true aficionados of the sport who provide not only the audience, albeit sometimes pitifully small, but more important, the betting market which determines the odds at which wagers are settled in the thousands of off-course betting shops. But while the racegoer is likely to be a punter, his adrenalin flows not simply from betting, but from the drama, the colour, the atmosphere and the excitement to be found on each and every one of the sixty courses in Britain. Be it the pageantry of Royal Ascot, the elegance of Goodwood or the rustic charm of a little jumping course, a Day at the Races has a magic all its own. Superb television coverage of the sport has given racing a bigger audience than it has ever had, but however excellent the cameramen and the commentators, they will never capture the full flavour which comes

from standing at the paddock rail watching a parade of fine, fit thoroughbreds. Or by a steeplechase fence when the birch is flying, and half a dozen horses are in the air together, straining every muscle as their jockeys seek to gain that extra yard, and land running at thirty miles or so an hour.

It is the heady exhilaration of such atmosphere which encourages otherwise sober, calculating, prudent citizens to throw discretion to the wind as they seek even closer involvement with the sport and take their first faltering steps towards possessing at least a part of a racehorse. For owners come from the ranks of racegoers, and while not all those who pay their way through the turnstiles will realize their ambition, few will not aspire to seeing their colours carried to victory at Epsom, Cheltenham or Bangor-on-Dee. To racegoers the horse is not just a line of type in the newspaper, a dot on the card, or a slot in the wheel of equine roulette, but half a ton of flesh, blood, bone and muscle, to be admired, respected, even revered. They see each horse as an individual, a character in his own right who can be as confident and sure of his own ability as was the mighty Arkle, as brave as Aldaniti, or as surly and unco-operative as others whose names are best forgotten.

There is too a generosity of spirit among racegoers which distinguishes them from the crowds who gather for other spectator sports. Perhaps it is a bond forged in sharing with others the triumph of victory or the adversity of defeat, even disaster. It is the character which develops

from winning occasionally and losing frequently with equanimity. The camaraderie among racegoers unites queens and commoners, millionaires and dustmen. Social barriers disappear fast when it comes to talk of horses, their performances and their prospects.

When the Racegoers' Club was founded in 1968 one of its first outings abroad was to America for the Washington DC International. It chartered a Boeing 707, and 150 members assembled at Heathrow. A motley crew they were too! A sprinkling from the pages of Debrett, a few from the very opposite end of the social scale, and the remainder a cross-section of everything in between.

Lord Kilmany, a senior member of both the Jockey Club and the Horserace Betting Levy Board, arrived with his wife. So did a couple of Irish navvies whose only address

was c/o George Wimpey, Cullompton Bypass. It seemed an unlikely mix for a four-day tour, potentially even disastrous. Whether the fact that a TWA Boeing on a transatlantic flight had never previously been known to run out of gin before it reached the Scilly Isles had anything to do with it is unclear, but by the time the plane landed at Dulles Airport 'Bill' Kilmany, Mick and Paddy were on Christian-name terms, and were to remain that way over many a hamburger for the rest of the trip.

Such is the true fellowship of the turf. Put any mixture of racegoers together and good-natured argument, cheerful banter and an abundance of stories will result.

They make their own stories too. Another Racegoers' Club trip to America involved a flight from New York to Miami, through a terrifying electric storm. The consumption of dry martinis was nearly, but not quite, halted when a stewardess on her first flight became hysterical with fear. Consumption stopped completely when the plane suddenly dropped several hundred feet and the martinis hit the roof. A deathly silence followed, broken only by Newmarket trainer Derek Weeden inquiring in hushed and respectful tones: 'What comes after "Hallowed by Thy name?" '

Had he thought a little he would have remembered the Irish priest who announced to his congregation one Summer Sabbath that 'Today is the last Sunday before Ascot,' and then forgot himself so much during the Lord's Prayer as to say 'Thy will be done on earth, as it was at Epsom.'

GLOSSARY

TO HORSE! TO HORSE!

Books of great learning invariably contain a glossary, published as an appendix to the text, which explains to the reader those terms, the very use of which throughout the chapters demonstrates the scholarship of the author. Clearly a book such as this should be no exception, but rather than cause constant reference to the last few pages, the explanation of the more common technical terms is included here, before we hit any of the trickier stuff. This also has the advantage of providing the reader with a few phrases of instant racing jargon with which to impress his audience when discussing a particularly trappy handicap, the form for which seems all up the spout because a doggy maiden pecked badly last time out when his conditional pilot took off too soon!

BIRTHDAYS

Age, sex, and marital status are usually a fairly straightforward business. Not so with horses. To begin with, they all have the same birthday, and on 1 January each year the entire horse population is instantly one year older, irrespective of whether they first saw the light of day on an icy January morning or a warm May evening. Because of this, horse births are controlled carefully, and a normally happy event would be anything but if it occurred at the end of December. Under such circumstances the animal's first birthday would come within a few days of foaling, and it would become a two-year-old, the minimum racing age, within thirteen months.

BREEDING SEASON

The breeding season is between January and June, and within this bracket foals can be described as 'early' or 'late'. This is particularly important during the first two racing seasons, when a 'late foal' can be at a considerable disadvantage compared with its so-called contemporaries in terms of strength and development. This situation can be further confused by the fact that horses may be early or late developers, and therefore more or less likely to race successfully in the early part of the season.

From the date of birth to the following 1 January the babies remain *foals*. For the next twelve months they are *yearlings*, and on their second New Year's Day become *two year-olds*.

GENDER OF HORSES

Foals and yearlings can be of either sex: the fellers are *colts* and the girls, *fillies*. However, when a colt reaches the age of five he becomes a *horse*, and may be referred to as an *entire*, provided, of course, that the vet hasn't got at him to remove the naughty bits which would enable him to enjoy fatherhood. If that should happen he becomes a *gelding*, and thwarted parental ambitions are then likely to be diverted into the more hazardous business of hurdling or steeplechasing. A few entire horses do compete over obstacles, and the more sensible ones are often seen to be jumping rather higher over the birch and gorse than the less vulnerable geldings. A filly, when she reaches the age of five, becomes a *mare*.

MAIDENS AND NOVICES

The term *maiden* has nothing whatever to do with gender. It applies to horses of both sexes which have not won a race. Hence special 'maiden' races, and 'maiden' allowances which are weight concessions for hitherto unsuccessful runners which compete against previous winners. A winner on the flat can still be a maiden over the jumps, and vice versa. However, just to confuse the issue, newcomers to the jumping game are referred to as *novices*, but while all novices start as maidens they remain novices until the end of the season in which they win their first race. And even winners over hurdles revert to novice status when they tackle the more formidable steeplechase fences.

Occasionally rather less complimentary names get attached to horses, and a *dog* or a *rogue* is probably best left out of calculations, indicating, as it does, unreliability, lack of co-operation, bad temper or similar unattractive qualities. On the other hand, *a proper Christian* will possess all the qualities you could wish for – and, hopefully, the ability to go with them.

RIDERS

Jockeys attached to flat-racing stables start their careers as *apprentices*. When they have acquired the basic skills, the trainer may give them the opportunity of race-riding, and in all but the more valuable races, and races confined to apprentice riders, they will receive the appropriate 'apprentice' allowance. This is a weight concession which varies according to the number of winners they have ridden. Until they have ten victories to their credit their allowance is seven pounds. This is reduced to five pounds until they have won 50 races, and then to three pounds until they get to 75 victories – at which time they have to take on Lester Piggott on equal terms!

Young steeplechase and hurdle jockeys do not serve an apprenticeship in quite the same way as their flat-racing counterparts, and *over the sticks* the youthful inexperienced rider is called a *conditional jockey*; he receives a seven-pound allowance until he has ridden fifteen winners, and one of four pounds until he has won thirty races.

Apprentices and conditional jockeys, like many inexperienced amateur riders, are sometimes referred to as *chalk-jockeys* – an

allusion to the fact that while racecourses have most jockey's names neatly painted on panels ready for inclusion on the runners-and-riders board, newcomers will find their names written up in chalk until the racecourse management reckons they will be regular-enough competitors to be worthy of the signwriter's skill.

RULES OF RACING: ENTRIES AND PRIZE-MONEY

It helps to understand a little of the administrative machinery which day in and day out ensures that horses appear on the racecourses. This, too, has a language of its own.

For most races *entries* are made, usually by the trainer, about one month before the race, although in some cases entries will close very much earlier. The Derby, for example, which is run at the beginning of June, closes in the previous November. Such events may have several *forfeit* stages, which means that horses can be withdrawn, or *scratched*, but the owners lose the entry fees they have already shelled out. However, at each forfeit stage the owners with horses remaining in the race must pay an additional fee for the privilege. All races have a final declaration stage four days before the race when the last of the fees are paid. Thereafter horses can only be taken out up to 10.00am (11am in winter) on the morning prior to the race; this is the *overnight stage*, at which point the final list of runners is compiled.

Most races are advertised with *added prize money*. This is the cash put up by the racecourse, the sponsor or the Levy Board – sometimes a combination of all three – which is added to the *sweepstakes pool* created by the owners' entry fees and forfeits. Taking the 1982 Derby as an illustration, the race was originally advertised as having £100,000 added prize money. When entries closed in November 1981 there were 288 possible runners, for each of which the entry fee of £400 had been paid. At the first forfeit stage on 20 April, 141 horses were taken out, the owners forfeiting only their original entry fees. The remaining 147 paid an additional £100 to stay in. On 18 May another 109 came out, and their owners lost £500 each. Only 38 horses were left in, and their optimistic owners paid an additional £400. At the four-day stage the field was reduced to 20, each of whose owners had then paid a total of £1,000 to get his horse into the Epsom line-up. Just two came out 'overnight', leaving the final field of 18 runners.

Although the race was advertised at £100,000 added, the total prize money, by the time the owners' cash was added to the pool, amounted to £247,100. Of this the winning owner got 46.5 per cent or £113,901: the owner of the second, 19.24 per cent or £46,542: the owner of the third, 9.57 per cent or £22,647, and the owner of the fourth, 4.61 per cent or £10,391. The winning trainer, Vincent O'Brien, earned 6 per cent and the winning jockey, Pat Eddery, 4.48 per cent, with the trainers and jockeys of the other placed horses receiving smaller amounts. The successful stables also benefitted from the prize money, while finally some small deduction was made for apprentice training and jockeys' valets.

These percentages vary slightly according to the type of race, but in no case does the winning owner receive as much as 60 per cent of the prize money. Of course, in a race like the Derby the prize money is almost irrelevant in that the winner is immediately one of the most valuable stallion prospects in the world, and likely to be worth several million pounds. One owner a few years ago was so delighted to win the Derby that he gave the whole of his share of the prize money to his jockey.

TYPES OF RACE

There is, however, only one Derby and four other *Classic* races each year, all of them confined to three year-olds. They are the 1,000 Guineas and the Oaks, which are restricted to fillies, and the 2,000 Guineas and the St Leger which, like the Derby, are open to both colts and fillies, although in practice few fillies run against the colts in these races. The Classics form part of a select group of prestigious events known as *Pattern Races*. There are about a hundred of these in Britain every year, and they in turn form part of the *European Pattern*, a carefully constructed framework of races designed to provide horses of all ages and sexes with a logical sequence of races over different distances, culminating in true championship events.

One step down from the Pattern Races, sometimes known as *Group Races* because they are divided into three categories according to their importance and prize-money

levels, are another hundred or so *Listed Races*. These are of lesser importance but of some significance to the breeding industry, and winning one of them can make a considerable difference to the value of the horse.

Whatever the quality of the race it is essential that the would-be punter understands its *conditions*. Of fundamental importance is the weight to be carried by each horse. In *Handicaps*, the official Jockey Club handicapper will have allotted varying weights to all the runners in an attempt to equalize their chances. Thus the best horse in a handicap field may be made to carry 10 stone, which includes the jockey, his saddlery and whatever amount of lead is necessary to bring him up to this weight, while a horse of lesser ability may only be asked to carry 7 stone 7 pounds. It is generally reckoned that over five furlongs, four pounds will make a difference of about a length. Over longer distances the effect will be greater, and in a two-mile race four pounds can mean a difference of four lengths. This is not an exact science because so many other factors are involved, but it is the principle worked on when making a handicap, and consequently it is theoretically possible through weight allocation to engineer a dead-heat between two horses which, if they were each carrying the same weight, would finish 35 lengths apart.

Handicappers remain steadfastly human, and because of the other factors such as the state of the ground, the relative strengths of the horses involved, and the tactics of the jockeys, punters will argue for hours and study the form book for clues as to why one horse is *better-in* a handicap than his rivals.

Non-handicap races are *Conditions Races*, and in these all horses start on level terms, though allowances may be given to those which have not won previously, or penalties allocated to those which have. There can be age and sex allowances too, but essentially all such races are designed to ensure that the best horse on the day wins the race.

Selling Races are generally for the poorer-quality horses and are so called because the winner is auctioned immediately after the race. In the past these races were frequently used to bring off some massive gambles when a horse of undoubted but publicly unexposed ability would be backed confidently to beat his untalented rivals. This happens less today, but trainers like Pat Rohan can still make the bookies wince from time to time, and while it is not generally advisable to bet in such races it can be worthwhile taking an interest when the betting market indicates that a horse is being backed heavily.

Auction Races are for horses which have been bought at public auction and which are allocated a racing weight in accordance with the price paid at the auction. Thus the most expensive purchase will carry the highest weight, the cheapest horse, the lightest.

EQUIPMENT

The equipment worn by horses in a race need not be of great concern to the racegoer or punter. Variations in

bits and bridles are either a matter of fashion, personal preference of the trainer, or specially devised to cater for the peculiarities of a particular horse. The exception is the *hood* or *blinkers* which must be declared at the overnight stage and will therefore be indicated in the newspapers and on the racecourse numbers board.

Some horses will show their best form only when wearing blinkers, which restrict a horse's vision so that it can see forwards but not to the side or backwards. This concentrates the horse's mind on the direction in which it is going and is particularly beneficial when used on animals which are put off their stride when another horse appears alongside, or seem reluctant to battle when challenged by other runners. A hood, which may or may not have blinkers attached to it, covers the ears and can be used with cotton wool to prevent the noise of a racecourse from distracting the horse.

GLOSSARY

As for the rest of the equipment, it is as well to know that *irons* mean stirrups, *leathers* are the straps which fasten the stirrups to the saddle, and that a sheepskin *noseband* is there not for decoration or to keep the horse warm, but to keep his head down. A *plate* has three meanings. In slang terms it can mean the saddle; more commonly it is one of the lightweight shoes – hence *spreading a plate*, which means the distortion of the shoe as it breaks away from the hoof. The third meaning is a race in which the total prize money is guaranteed, but owners' entry fees and forfeits are not added. This is restricted largely to race meetings run in aid of charity, where a sponsor puts up the prize money and the charity benefits from the entry fees.

A similar principle is more common

in less valuable races known as *Guaranteed Sweepstakes*.

UNDERSTANDING THE COMMENTATORS

It is in descriptions of races that the jargon can be at its most mystifying. A young horse can run *green*, meaning that it shows signs of inexperience; it can be *on the bit*, or restrained by the jockey in the early part of the race to prevent it running too freely, thereby using up its energy before the jockey *asks the question*, when the final effort is required. Once *given its head*, or *let down*, it is said to be *off the bit!* It can *change legs*, meaning that a horse changes its action, and having been leading its stride with its right leg switches to the left or vice versa. It can *take the ground* of another horse by crossing in front of it, and if in doing so it interferes with the chances of the other horse a disqualification is automatic. Other offences which will lead to disqualification are *bumping*; and *boring* when one horse leans into another. In steeplechasing and hurdling a horse may be seen to *peck*

on landing over an obstacle – a mistake which results in the horse's nose almost touching the ground, but from which it recovers to continue in the race, often with little ill-effect.

In-and-out running refers to a lack of consistency in the form of a horse shown in a number of races – unreliability which should ring warning bells for punters thinking of backing the beast. Running *in snatches* means inconsistency of running in one race, the horse going well one minute but idling the next.

Commentators will sometimes refer to *the distance, the distance marker* or *the distance pole*. This is shortly before the start of the final furlong of a race, 240 yards from the winning post. However, if a horse wins by *a distance* it means it has won by more than 30 lengths. If it fails to *get the distance*, it means that it is unable to stay the course at racing pace, either because it is not fully fit, or because it needs a shorter *trip* to be seen to best advantage. A tired horse can be said to *hang under pressure* when it veers to one side or the other, sometimes *hanging away from the whip*, sometimes *hanging into the whip*. When this happens a skilful jockey will pull his whip through to the other hand and straighten his horse, hopefully before causing interference with another runner.

TO HORSE! TO HORSE!

The Owner wears a hat. Although in cases of the more eccentric racing nobility, The Hat appears to wear the Owner. Owners' hats are invariably soft, brown and suffering. A nasty case, I'd say, your Honour, of GBH – Grievous Bodily Hat.

Owners' hats may be doffed, for ladies or passing Royalty. They may be hurled in the air, but only at Cheltenham, and then only if they're Irish. Otherwise they are *never* removed. Some sages of the Turf will hold that the Hat stays Pat, even to the extent of Bath, Bed and Ablutions.

Owners are thin, ascetic, rangy even. They wear tweed suits with turnups on their trousers, which in turn are slightly too short to reach their heavy brogue shoes, which used to be brown, once. Only in sub-arctic conditions, such as are encountered at Cheltenham in spring or Newmarket in summer, do they wear an outer protective garment. This invariably takes the form of an old, lovat-green coat, heavily soup-stained, with a nasty droop in one shoulder, weighed down over the years by heavy racing-glasses.

The owner's tipple is champagne before breakfast, and pink gin thereafter. His complexion, however, remains aristocratically pale. This despite constant exposure to the worst of the elements in such far-flung reaches of the Empire as Uttoxeter and Haydock. Owners have a slight stoop, from bending down to talk to jockeys, and an aloof expression from ignoring other owners, and the advice of their trainer.

Although the owner's hat conceals a high forehead and his conversation is liberally doused with references to Keynes, Nietzsche and Jung, the pale eyes beneath are vague. They seem to look beyond you, at a point distant from the ken of other mortals. One feels inadequate in the presence of an owner. His pre-occupation is with another horizon. Something finer, nobler. The horse. His horse. His dream. There are no other horses but his. It may eat the owner out of house and home, and run every Selling Handicap like an octogenarian going round a hypermarket, but one day, some day soon, it will stalk, proudly steaming, into the winner's enclosure, the owner's wife will pat it gingerly on the head, withdrawing her hand quickly lest it have her fingers off, Lord Oaksey will doff *his* hat, while presenting the trophy, and the owner can die happy . . . .

Racehorse owners in Britain come in all shapes, sizes, ages, sexes, colours, and most of what the ad-men call sociological groups. They have, however, one thing in common – an uncontrollable urge to spend money in a frenzy of financial masochism, tinged with an absurdly British spirit of optimism which assumes insuperable odds are there only to be overcome. After all, Drake finished a game of bowls before knocking the Spanish Armada bandy, and a few apparently scatterbrained Spitfire pilots did much the same to the might of the Luftwaffe.

Racehorse owners are of that breed. They will spend anything from a few hundred pounds to upwards of a quarter of a million to acquire their pride and joy. When it costs a fortune they will justify their extravagance with the thought that it is 'beautifully bred, sure to be a Derby prospect', or, when rather less expensive, with the self-satisfaction which admits that 'it's not fashionably bred, but has outstanding conformation and is the sort to beat the best of them'.

But whether the beast in question is top-drawer or bargain-basement, it will require of its PO (Proud Owner) a further investment of about £8,000 a year. Even if the PO is unsure which end the expensive oats go in, one thing is absolutely certain. They will go in. And so will the best hay and an awful lot of other things regardless of whether the said beast becomes a champion or sinks into the obscurity to which most are destined. What's more, regardless of its eventual talent, it will need to be groomed, exercised, shod and mucked out. And the prices for all those things don't vary according to the ability of the animal.

That, give or take a few bob, means the said PO has to shell out about a hundred and fifty quid a week until he becomes a VPO (Very Proud Owner), who leads in a winner, or degenerates to being a POO (Pissed-Off Owner) who goes back to breeding ferrets.

The £150 a week doesn't all go in keep and training, of course. Only most of it. The rest is spent on the PO's behalf in entry fees for races, transporting the horse to the

TO HORSE! TO HORSE!

course, and jockeys' fees, for which the owner can expect some predictable albeit professional advice: 'Sure to win a little race sometime, Sir, if you run him over a shorter/ longer trip on firmer/softer going, on a left-hand/right-hand course or he is ridden from the front/behind.' Occasionally, after all these permutations have been exhausted, more realistic words may follow on the lines of: 'Might be as well to cut your losses, Sir.' But, rest assured, *that* is likely to be many weeks and many £150s later.

Owners, by and large, know all this before they produce their cheque books, but optimism will always outweigh logic, and the prospect of getting hold of a good 'un will always be more attractive than accepting the reality that 95 per cent of all horses in training will show a loss.

For those fortunate few who do hit the jackpot, the rewards are immense. Take, for example, George Moore, something of a tycoon in the furniture trade whose knowledge of racing was a good deal less than his understanding of consumer preferences in kitchen cupboards. However, George, a canny Yorkshireman, saw dividends to be had from running a horse which could carry the name of his domestic woodwork. Furthermore, he reasoned, it would give his workforce an added interest, his sales reps a talking point, and, who knows, the company might just make a few quid on the deal.

Luckily for Mr Moore, whose knowledge of horses was such that one of his first questions was to ask where his animal should be 'garaged', he sought the advice of Lester Piggott's better half, Susan, whose bloodstock agency invested a modest 4,000 guineas in a colt which 'might do the job'.

Moorestyle, as the purchase was called, was sent, somewhat incestuously, to Susan's brother Robert Armstrong to be turned into a racehorse, and after winning more or less everything there was to be won between five and seven furlongs, has finished up with a not-unattractive life of limited but lucrative purpose at the National Stud. Quite apart from the prize money of £302,411 won over three seasons, Mr Moore finally sold a large part of his shareholding in Moorestyle to the Nation when the horse was valued at £2.2 million. This was a lower sum, let it be said, than the patriotic Yorkshireman could have obtained from the stallion-hungry syndicates of Kentucky.

But Moorestyle was a fairytale come true. More typical was Terry's experience with Wogan's Wager, the saga of which is detailed in the next chapter.

It would be cynical to suggest that owners' motives are purely financial. The fascination of ownership goes far deeper. For many there is the inexplicable joy of association with a beautiful animal, whatever its ability. Watching it develop from an excitable, often unco-ordinated baby, to a finely-tuned athlete, suffering its ailments, rejoicing in its progress, charting its development, and sharing with its trainer the thrills of expectation and the despondency which all too often

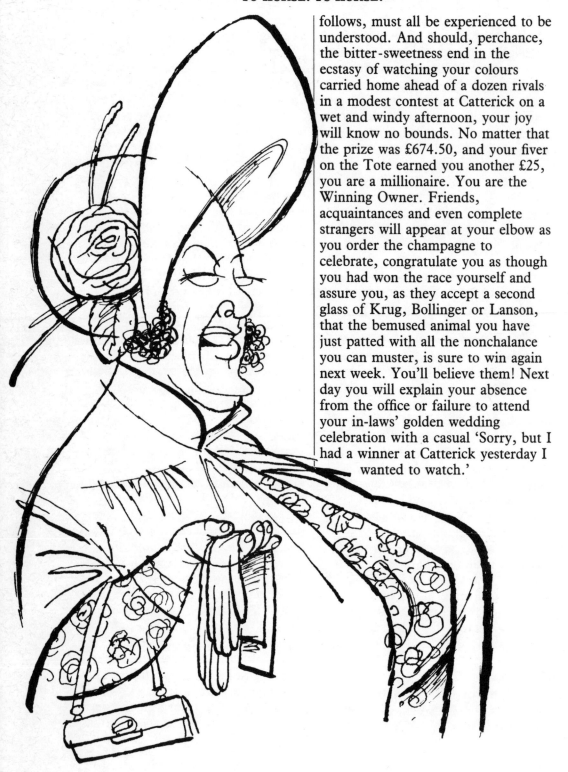

follows, must all be experienced to be understood. And should, perchance, the bitter-sweetness end in the ecstasy of watching your colours carried home ahead of a dozen rivals in a modest contest at Catterick on a wet and windy afternoon, your joy will know no bounds. No matter that the prize was £674.50, and your fiver on the Tote earned you another £25, you are a millionaire. You are the Winning Owner. Friends, acquaintances and even complete strangers will appear at your elbow as you order the champagne to celebrate, congratulate you as though you had won the race yourself and assure you, as they accept a second glass of Krug, Bollinger or Lanson, that the bemused animal you have just patted with all the nonchalance you can muster, is sure to win again next week. You'll believe them! Next day you will explain your absence from the office or failure to attend your in-laws' golden wedding celebration with a casual 'Sorry, but I had a winner at Catterick yesterday I wanted to watch.'

THE OWNER

The marriage vow 'With all my worldly goods, I thee endow' does not always extend to the owning of racehorses, and occasionally husbands and wives will maintain separate racing establishments.

One such couple were the Taylors – 'EP', the famous Canadian millionaire, and his wife. Their horses met in competition from time to time and EP tended to get the best of the arguments. On one occasion after his horse had finished a short head in front of his wife's, he received a cable from an English friend which read: 'Stop beating your wife.' Undeterred he replied immediately: 'At least I do it in public!'

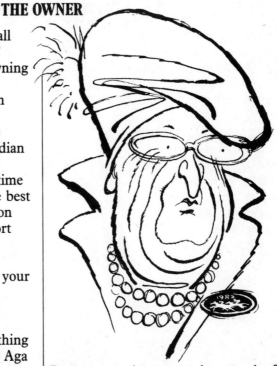

In ownership, as in everything else, success is relative. HH The Aga Khan and pools magnate Robert Sangster will probably need a rather better excuse than Catterick for absenting themselves from the spiritual duties associated with the leader of 20 million Moslems, or from the demands of scrutinizing the 150 million Xs on the weekly football coupons. But substitute Epsom, Ascot, Newmarket or York for Catterick and the excuse will be equally valid.

How then, does one join this seemingly élite corps of super-optimists ready to hazard so much in search of so few elusive moments of elation? Although it helps to have the resources of an Arabian oil sheikh, an acre or two of real estate in Mayfair, or the proceeds of an unsolved bank robbery to back up the fantasy, racehorse owning is, surprisingly perhaps, within the reach of more people today then ever before.

Recent years have seen the growth of partnerships and syndicates, and with them the spread of ownership from newspaper proprietors to newsagents, from oil tycoons to the forecourt attendants on their filling stations. For while it may cost £4,000 to buy the beast, and twice as much again each year to keep it, bills of even that size can be met easily enough by a dozen people each of whom is prepared to forego 20 cigarettes and a couple of pints of beer a day.

To help offset the fearsome costs of keeping this would-be Derby winner in training, the prospective owner might calculate that even after the jockeys and trainers have had their whack of the spoils, there is upwards of £11 million to be won each year in prize money. With 12,000 horses in training, that averages nearly £1,000 a horse. But he must be warned. Averages are deceptive. The top 5 per cent of owners win 80 per cent of the money, which leaves precious little for the rest, and more than half the owners with nothing at all.

However, faint heart never won Black Beauty, so the logical reasoning processes which normally govern investment opportunities are best forgotten. Instead, the purchase price and training costs should be

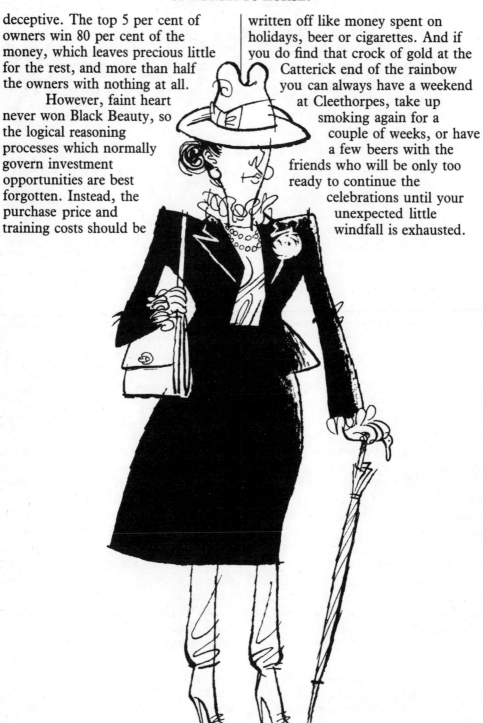

written off like money spent on holidays, beer or cigarettes. And if you do find that crock of gold at the Catterick end of the rainbow you can always have a weekend at Cleethorpes, take up smoking again for a couple of weeks, or have a few beers with the friends who will be only too ready to continue the celebrations until your unexpected little windfall is exhausted.

TERRY WOGAN

THE HORSE OR WAGAN'S WOGER

TO HORSE! TO HORSE!

It's a lonely life, here at the bottom of the *Sporting Life* Tipsters' League, and I must admit to moments of real heartbreak and torment, when I am as near as a toucher to burning my form book, Lord Oaksey's Guide To What The Well-Dressed Toff Is Wearing, and e'en granny's old magic hat-pin . . . .

For I seem to be the only living Irishman who's not an expert on horseflesh, and who doesn't clean out the bookies every time he sets foot on a racecourse. I've never been to a meeting yet where I didn't bequeath my hard-earned to the turf accountants. They see me coming a long way off, and start making excited signs to one another. Many people think that this signalling is a code, to communicate the odds on the various horses to each other. Not so. What they're signalling is the joyous message: 'He's here again! The Mug. Whoopee! Tonight we eat!'

I'm not a complete goodaw, amadan or eejit when it comes to horses, you know. It's just that, rightly or wrongly, I've always been a little timid of anything that stands about 12 feet tall, with lots of iron-shod legs, and teeth like Julio Iglesias. The breath's nothing to write home about either.

'Never show fear,' warn horsey friends. 'They can smell it!' I'll bet they can, and they're good judges. Horses show a regrettable tendency to roll the whites of their eyes, and go for me like a bucket of best nuts. That's not to say that I haven't shown one or two of the creatures just who's the boss. We

Wogans are a hardy breed, and at our most dangerous when challenged. Who was it showed a couple of cow-ponies the ropes, round the rugged landscape of Yosemite National Park, California, last summer? Who was it wouldn't have gone within a mile of a cow-pony, if his eight-year-old daughter hadn't shamed him into it?

I could do with more horses like those cow-ponies. Imperturbable, cat-footed, they picked their way down rocky escarpments, across river beds, around steep dusty trails, responding gallantly to the master-horseman's every delicate touch and command. Or so the master-horseman liked to think. In fact, the foxy little horses are so used to the trail that they know every hoofmark backwards and blindfolded. You can do what you like with your reins, knees, heels or hands, they'll take you there and bring you back. Indeed, if you fell off they'd probably carry you back to the stables in their teeth, like a faithful retriever.

Wogan's Wager was much like a cow-pony; about the same size, and he ran a bit like one, too. I always felt that he would have been much more at home trekking gently through forests and over dusty trails, rather than chasing gamely after horses that were much bigger, and faster, than he was.

I only had a small share in him, half a hock I think it was, but the syndicate of which I was part named the unfortunate little animal after me. Small wonder if its growth was stunted.

Wogan's Wager had a couple of runs, without ever breaking into a

sweat, not to mind a hand-canter, before I went to see him race for the first time 'neath the ancient Roman walls of historic Chester, on the famed Roodeye. The trainer had an air of quiet confidence, which he hardily maintained right up to the moment when the little horse strolled nonchalantly out of the starting-gate, and loped easily into a position about 100 yards behind the rest of the field. He was never troubled, and finished pulling-up, a comfortable last. He was a true Corinthian, that horse. He enjoyed the day out, the fun of it all, the camaraderie of the stables. For him, it was not the winning that counted, just the joy of taking part.

I might have enjoyed it more, if the race commentator hadn't persistently referred to the horse throughout the race as 'Wagan's Woger'. On dark nights as I toss and turn, I can still hear the jeering and ribald chaffing of the crowd.

The jockey was confident afterwards: 'Oh yes, Sir, he'll win a few, never fear.' He did, too. *After* I sold my interest in him, the little rascal won four out of his five races, at 25–1, 10–1, 11–8 and 9–4. I didn't have a bet on any of them. Just call me Lucky Wogan . . . .

TERRY WOGAN

THE TRAINER

TO HORSE! TO HORSE!

The trainer wears a hat on course, and a cap on the job. He is a man of lowly stature, having once been a jockey himself. If he was once a *jump*-jockey, of course, he may scale the dizzy heights of as much as 5ft 10in, and wear the bemused expression of one who has ridden around Aintree once too often.

The trainer is the last remaining link with the Middle Ages, running his establishment in the time-honoured fashion of the feudal baron. His yard resembles nothing so much as the castle keep, with wenches, serfs, yeomen, squires and knights abounding. The wenches and serfs are the stable lads and lasses, working all the hours God sends for a pittance and lodgings. The yeomen are the blacksmiths and the other skilled tradesmen, proud, independent, but fiercely loyal to their lord and master. The squires are the apprentice jockeys, and the knights are the jockeys themselves, on the choicest steeds, decked out in their lord's livery as they ride to death or glory. And it can come pretty close to death, if they don't follow the trainer's instructions to the letter!

Trainers are hard taskmasters, having endured the hardships of the yard in their own apprenticeships. They carry riding crops, in the manner of Reichsmarschalls or plantation owners, smacking them impatiently against their riding boots when thwarted, or infuriated by yet another inanity from some unfortunate owner. Indeed, it is the opinion of most trainers that theirs would be a pretty fine life

if it wasn't for the owners. Owners make crazy demands, such as insisting that their horses run at race-meetings. They *even* expect the things to *win*, and become petulant when they don't!

It is mainly because of owners that the trainer's stern martinet-like expression is tempered by an air of saintly forbearance. His eyebrows arch, from looking heavenwards for guidance and patience in dealing with all morons, and particularly those who know Nothing About Racing. Which is everybody from the Jockey Club down, not excluding God.

Trainers smoke Havana cigars and drink Dom Perignon '71 when

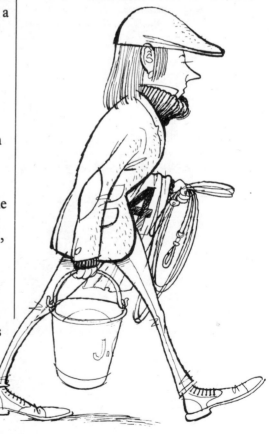

THE TRAINER

their horses win, and the same when they don't. For it is Never the Trainer's Fault! The horse loses because of a combination of factors beyond any trainer's control, such as the going, the jockey, the handicapper, the judge, the weather, the wife, the wind, indigestion, but usually the owner, for insisting the horse runs at all, when he obviously wasn't *ready*! Only trainers know when horses are ready; and *when* they're ready, and *only* when they're ready, do they *win*.

Just don't expect to be told about it beforehand, that's all . . . .

TONY FAIRBAIRN

Trainers roll out of bed shortly before most self-respecting sparrows have even thought about their morning ablutions, and crawl back into it after a sixteen or seventeen hour day. In between times they look after several dozen temperamental thoroughbreds, their even more temperamental owners, a business turnover running into hundreds of thousands of pounds each year, the attendant paper work, and, for good measure, notch up thirty or forty thousand miles a year behind the wheel of a car, as they drive to racecourses all over the country.

It's a grand life, is that of a trainer – provided you have the stamina of a Grand National winner, the versatility of a pentathlete, the tenacity of an income-tax inspector, the charm of Angela Rippon, and the driving technique of James Hunt.

Curiously enough, the time spent in actually training the horses occupies a relatively small proportion of the long day, but deciding the work programme for each horse, first to get it fit and then to produce it at its peak on the racecourse on a given day, calls for a combination of skills which, in the case of the most successful, goes beyond flair and into the realms of genius.

Flat-race trainers will usually meet most of their charges for the first time in the late autumn when they have been bought – generally by the trainer himself – at the yearling sales. Others will be sent to him by owners direct from the stud at which they were bred. In either event, the trainer's first job is to 'break' the animal, a misnomer if ever there was one, for persuading an excitable young animal who has spent the past eighteen months enjoying the freedom and sunshine of the paddocks that its role in life is to be bridled, saddled and ridden by man calls for patience, understanding and kindness. Without the benefit of these, the chances that the horse will demonstrate Christian qualities and co-operation during its racing life are remote.

Once the yearlings are broken in, their real training starts. Gently at first, just walking and occasionally trotting round the trainer's paddocks. This teaches them the rudiments of their job and to respond to the commands of their rider expressed through his hands and heels. Cantering and roadwork follow to build up their strength, and by the New Year they may well be ready to canter up the gallops in groups of three or four to give them some idea of what will be expected of them on the racecourse.

Horses can be made fit – and kept fit – without having to gallop all over the training grounds as though the hounds of hell were behind them, and fast work is the final stage of preparation used to bring them to peak condition, assess their ability, and clear the wind.

While all this is going on, probably for six months or more, the trainer will be monitoring the progress of each of his horses, watching their muscular development, keeping a careful eye open for physical problems, and deciding upon their likely capability. This is where the skill of a trainer counts, for each horse in his charge is an individual to be treated as such if he is to reach his true potential. His work programme, his feed, his medication, all need careful analysis, and the consistently successful trainer is the one who couples this understanding with the flair and ability to do the right thing at the right time for each horse in his care. Many of the best-known trainers have between fifty and a hundred horses to look after – some even more – but to remain successful they can never introduce standard work programmes, and will never ignore the individual characteristics and requirements of their horses. Of course, trainers must rely heavily on the staff they employ, particularly their key man – the head lad.

He is the man who must carry out the orders of the trainer and take charge of the stable when the guvnor is away at the races, sometimes for several days at a stretch. The head lad is also responsible for feeding the horses, and a good head lad is worth his weight in prize money. The stable lads – another misnomer since many of them ride out until their pension books arrive – are nowadays a great deal better-paid as a result of minimum-wage agreements reached within the last ten years. However, it's a tough job involving a dawn start, a seven-days-a-week rota, and all the misery that freezing temperatures, biting winds and drenching rain can throw at man and horse high on the downs or in the middle of an open heath. But a good lad with a genuine feel for the two or three horses he looks after is an invaluable member of the team.

Apart from the inevitable paperwork associated with running a business employing perhaps forty or fifty people, the trainer must decide upon the racing programme of his horses. Entries will need to be made four or five weeks before the race, and because the trainer will want several alternative engagements for each horse so that he has a choice of going conditions, opposition and distance, he may well make six times as many entries as he has runners each week. Again this is where the successful trainer will demonstrate his skill, for finding the right race for his horse is an art which can ensure that even a moderate horse can be placed to win a race.

Sam Hall, the great Yorkshire trainer whose death in 1977 robbed the sport of one of its most splendid characters, was full of homespun philosophy and no little cunning when it came to winning races. 'Keep yourself in the best company and your horse in the worst,' he would say, and certainly he took his own advice, for however good he thought a horse might be, he would start its racing career in modest company and let it work its way up to take on the best. Operating in reverse, he believed, was time-consuming and expensive. He trained nine horses for the Racegoers' Club in the six years

before he died, and every one was a winner, yet none cost more than £2,000. The most successful, a little filly called Voucher Book, he bought for only 350 guineas, yet she won eight races. Nor was he slow to get rid of a horse in his care when it was costing the owner more than he could hope to recover. 'Better,' he would say, 'an empty house than a bad tenant.'

Another Racegoers' Club trainer was Doug Marks, ex-jockey, comedian, and racehorse trainer extraordinary to Jimmy Tarbuck and Frankie Vaughan. His wise words, when they could be sifted from non-stop wisecracks, related to the biggest problem faced by all trainers – owners. 'Owners,' maintained Doug, 'are fine. No problem at all – until they win a race. Then, God help you. They reckon it's easy from that moment on. They expect you to do it all the time, and they'll worry the life out of you if you don't.'

The popular owners among trainers are those who let the professional get on with the job, who don't ring up three times a week, who don't try and plan the horse's programme, and who never telephone for information about the other horses in the stable. A trainer with, perhaps, forty owners to deal with would have an impossible task if each of them telephoned every night to ask after their own horse and the prospects of three or four others due to race the next day. Yet it is amazing the number of owners who do believe they have some sort of divine right to be told every time a runner from the stable is fancied.

Of course, trainers expect to

contact their owners the day before a horse runs, and to report back after the race should the owner not be present. But that, too, is time-consuming, particularly if the trainer has several runners in an afternoon.

It is, clearly, much easier with telephones than it was in the old days, and the story is told of Sid Farell who trained in the early part of the century when he had among his owners a certain noble lord. This pillar of the aristocracy would visit Sid's yard every Friday evening to discuss the Saturday racing, and to plan the campaign for the week ahead. As he was also 'something in the City' he seldom got to the races in midweek, and when one of his horses ran Sid would send him a telegram report of the race. This tended to be a stride-by-stride account which was all very well, but the cost of the telegrams was put on his lordship's training bill. Eventually the owner remonstrated with his trainer. Telegram costs were getting out of hand, he explained, and would it be possible to cable only the basic facts.

The following week the peer received a telegram. It read 'S.F.S.F.S.F.S.F', and left him mystified. On the Friday evening he asked the trainer to explain. 'Brevity,' he said, 'is one thing. This is ridiculous.'

'Oh! I thought you would understand,' said Sid. 'S.F.S.F.S.F.S.F – it tells the whole story. Started, farted, slipped and fell, see you Friday, Sid Farell.'

TO HORSE! TO HORSE!

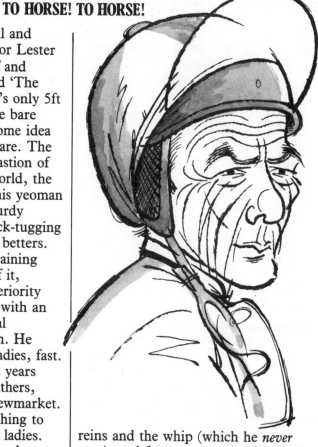

The jockey is small and gnarled. Except for Lester Piggott, who is *tall* and gnarled. He's called 'The Long Fella' and he's only 5ft 8in in his prehensile bare feet. Which will give you some idea of how small jockeys *really* are. The stable yard being the last bastion of feudalism in the Western world, the jockey still behaves as did his yeoman forefathers, combining a sturdy independence with a forelock-tugging obsequiousness towards his betters.

The jockey's early training and physical size, or lack of it, combine to give him an inferiority complex which he combats with an excessive cockiness or sexual precociousness, usually both. He likes his repartee, and his ladies, fast. His face is lined beyond his years through exposure to all weathers, particularly the winds of Newmarket. It's also probably got something to do with the aforementioned ladies. Jockeys are not just thin, they're emaciated. This, combined with their bandy legs (from years in the saddle) gives them the appearance of some under-nourished Third World child with rickets.

The little chap's skin is nut-brown, which is partly due to the bracing open air, but mostly to long holidays 'neath a Far Eastern or West Indian sun. His eyes are puckered and narrowed from peeking over horses' heads, and up other horses' backsides. This also accounts for the jockey's world-weary expression. The jockey, you feel, has seen it all. Probably more than is good for him. His hands, as you might expect, are hard and horny from gripping the reins and the whip (which he *never* uses), and from patting the flanks of horses, and, indeed, of women, to whom we have already made sufficient reference above.

The jockey carries himself with a spring in his step, like a man glad to have his feet on the ground, which in fact he is, having to spend much of his life uncomfortably perched on the back of some thoroughbred with a temperament like Attila the Hun. The rest of the time he's in mid-air, flying his own plane from Devon and Exeter to Ayr, or more conventionally jetting from Washington to Longchamp, from Florida to Hong Kong. His energy is prodigious and his health legendary, mainly because he doesn't smoke,

THE JOCKEY

drink, or eat. Not because he doesn't want to – he simply hasn't got the time.

The jockey likes people better than horses, stable lads better than trainers, trainers better than owners, owners better than Stewards of the Jockey Club, and children better than anything. At least, they can't talk down to him . . . .

Jockeys range in age from 16 to 66, and there's no way of telling the difference. They are born aged in the wood, and the passing years make no impression. When he's had enough of smiling at silly owners, and snarling at silly horses, the jockey retires to become a trainer, a best-selling author, or a television commentator. In the latter role, he has made a sterling contribution to the English language, by the complete annihilation of the letter 'g'. About time too . . . .

TONY FAIRBAIRN

A few years ago the Japanese staged a couple of jockeys' invitation races in Tokyo and Kyoto where, in front of their average Sunday race crowd of about 150,000 spectators, riders from Britain, Ireland, France, USA, Australia and Brazil got duffed up by the local lads who, by a stroke of oriental good fortune, managed to draw all the best horses in the ballot for mounts. Not that it mattered a damn, for a great time was had by all, and while national pride was satisfied in the land of the Rising Sun, no-one over the horizon took very much notice.

Nevertheless it was an interesting promotion, and in accordance with local custom a great deal more of the jockeys' time was spent at Press conferences than in race-riding.

The Japanese are not only extremely hospitable, they are intensely keen on fact-finding, sifting every shred of information which might be put to good use, and Press conferences, like Geisha parties, are all part of this process. Mostly the questions were predictable and the answers even more so. One, however, was fascinating.

'What importance do you world-class jockeys attach to your own skills in relation to the ability of

the horse when it comes to winning races?' One might have expected the jockeys to emphasize their own contribution as justification for the star treatment they were receiving, but in fact they were virtually unanimous in declaring that it was 95 per cent the ability of the horse and only 5 per cent the talent of the jockey when the chips were really down.

With European champions Willie Carson, Yves St Martin and Wally Swinburn Snr on the panel it would be a brave man who would argue, and yet on the face of it the riders themselves were minimizing their own importance. In fact what all these internationally acclaimed jockeys were saying was that the difference between the average professional and the top-class riders with that almost-indefinable star quality is measurable only in such fractional terms. No jockey, however talented, can conjure success from a horse without ability, while any competent jockey should be able to win on a horse which is superior to its rivals.

However, the vast majority of races are highly competitive contests between horses of approximately comparable ability, so that a variable 'jockeyship factor' of five per cent can be of paramount importance. It is hardly surprising therefore that in all the major racing countries the services of top-flight jockeys are highly sought-after, and the handful of international star performers are among the highest-paid of all professional sportsmen.

The successful jockey is supremely fit, possesses natural

THE JOCKEY

ability reinforced by experience, balance, judgment, tactical skill, patience, bravery, instinct, dedication and confidence. With an abundance of such qualities he will also need a first-class financial adviser, for he will have little time himself to nip into the post office to buy savings certificates or premium bonds.

Like trainers, jockeys start their day before sun-up, to be out on the training gallops in the misty early morning. Lester Piggott's breakfast of a cup of black coffee and a half corona is rather more spartan than most, but few jockeys can afford the calorific luxury of anything very much more substantial. Then it's back to the gallops for more work-riding before the daily drive to the racecourse and anything between one and six rides in the afternoon.

A professional jockey currently receives a fee of £29 for each flat race, or £39.50 for a steeplechase or hurdles race. The differential reflects the shorter career of the jump jockey, the greater hazards he faces, and the lower level of prize money generally in jumping which limits the percentage earned from riding a winner or a placed horse.

A winning jockey will receive between 4.48 and 6.93 per cent of the total prize money for the race. The scale, laid down in the Rules of Racing, varies between the flat and jumping and depends upon whether or not there is a fourth prize. The jockey finishing second usually receives fractionally less than one per cent and the third jockey home about half of one per cent.

The flat-race jockey will

benefit also from more rides than his jumping colleague. When Lester Piggott won the jockeys' championship in 1981, his 179 winners came from a total of 703 rides, whereas in the 1980–81 jumping season Johnnie Francome finished as top jockey with 105 winners from 574 rides. And in those same seasons the top twelve flat-race jockeys shared 1,133 winners, while the dozen top jump jockeys mustered only 696.

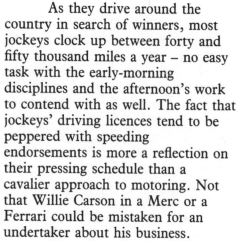

As they drive around the country in search of winners, most jockeys clock up between forty and fifty thousand miles a year – no easy task with the early-morning disciplines and the afternoon's work to contend with as well. The fact that jockeys' driving licences tend to be peppered with speeding endorsements is more a reflection on their pressing schedule than a cavalier approach to motoring. Not that Willie Carson in a Merc or a Ferrari could be mistaken for an undertaker about his business.

While most jockeys dislike the hours spent behind the wheel of a car, the most exhausting problem faced by many of them is the continuous struggle against increasing weight. Anyone who has battled for a week or two to shed half a stone of superfluous fat will know the misery it can cause. When there's no superfluous fat there in the first place, living like an undernourished sparrow in order to maintain a constantly spare frame is truly wretched. Diuretic pills and/or sweltering saunas combine to produce the ills of dehydration as a jockey seeks to weigh out at 7 stone 10 pounds when the Good Lord never intended him to be under 8 stone 5, and lucky indeed is the rider who, like Willie Carson, can perform impressively at the dinner table and still weigh out next day at 7 stone 9.

Riding accidents are another constant hazard faced by every jockey, and while flat racing is relatively accident-free, a fall in a flat race is likely to be more serious than over hurdles or fences where the pace is slower and the jockeys more prepared for a tumble. Indeed most jump jockeys expect to part company with their horses about once in every eight rides – and that at thirty miles an hour with half a ton or so of horse coming down with you is no joke. But the jump jockey is a hardy customer who dismisses a broken collar bone with a cheery wave of the other arm, a cracked rib with a wry smile rather than a hearty laugh and anything more serious as a frustrating inconvenience which will stop him falling off again for several weeks. Recent years have seen a considerable tightening of the rules and regulations covering a jockey's fitness to ride, particularly with regard to head injuries and concussion, and while a jockey who has been knocked unconscious, albeit briefly, may resent having to spend at least three days on the sidelines, his best interests are served by the stringent medical supervision to which he is now subjected.

Much has been written of the bravery of the jump-jockey – most of it dismissed by the jockeys themselves as emotional slush – but no chapter referring to them would be complete without a tribute to the way in which they accept the risks of their profession with equanimity, the battering of their bodies with stoicism, and their relatively small rewards with an infectious humour which singles them out from other professional sportsmen. They ride seventy or eighty miles a week over hurdles and fences at racing pace because they love it. They love their horses, they respect their fellow riders, and they live for their next ride. If they play as hard as they work, it is scarcely surprising, and they are none the worse for that.

Behind the seemingly taciturn appearance of Lester Piggott lies a highly engaging sense of humour which is at its most mischievous whenever money is involved. He has always given the impression that he is very much better at making the stuff than spending it, and although, quietly, he is as generous as the next man, he has acquired something of a Jack Benny image.

There is the well-known story of how a stable lad who had led up one of Lester's big-race winners failed to receive his tip from the jockey and reckoned that on a point of principle he should get a pound or two. Consequently, the next time Lester appeared in the yard the lad sidled up to him a little diffidently and mumbled something about 'the pound you owe me for leading up that winner'.

Lester, who is known to be a little hard of hearing, directed the plaintiff to his other ear and, encouraged by the absence of a total rebuff, the lad said, rather more loudly: 'Lester, what about the two quid you owe me for that winner?'

'Yeah,' murmured the champ, 'I heard you. But go back to the pound ear, it's cheaper.'

Another, probably apocryphal, story concerns the racing journalist who dropped into the habit some years ago of driving Lester between Newmarket and Doncaster whenever racing took place at the Yorkshire course. On the way back it was their custom to stop for a light meal, and the journalist found that he always paid the bill. As he provided the petrol too, he felt eventually that the time had come for Lester to make some contribution.

They arrived at their usual restaurant one evening, and at the end of the meal the waiter presented the writer with the bill neatly folded on a plate. Without picking it up, the scribe edged it gently towards the middle of the table. Lester ignored it and carried on their conversation. After waiting a few moments, the racing correspondent pushed it even closer to Lester who again appeared not to notice. This continued for several minutes until eventually the plate had been moved almost into Lester's lap. At that point the great man could ignore it no more and picking up the paper he unfolded it slowly, studied it carefully, refolded it, put it back on the plate and returned it to his long-standing host, observing only: 'I shouldn't pay all that if I were you.'

TERRY WOGAN

THE PUNTER

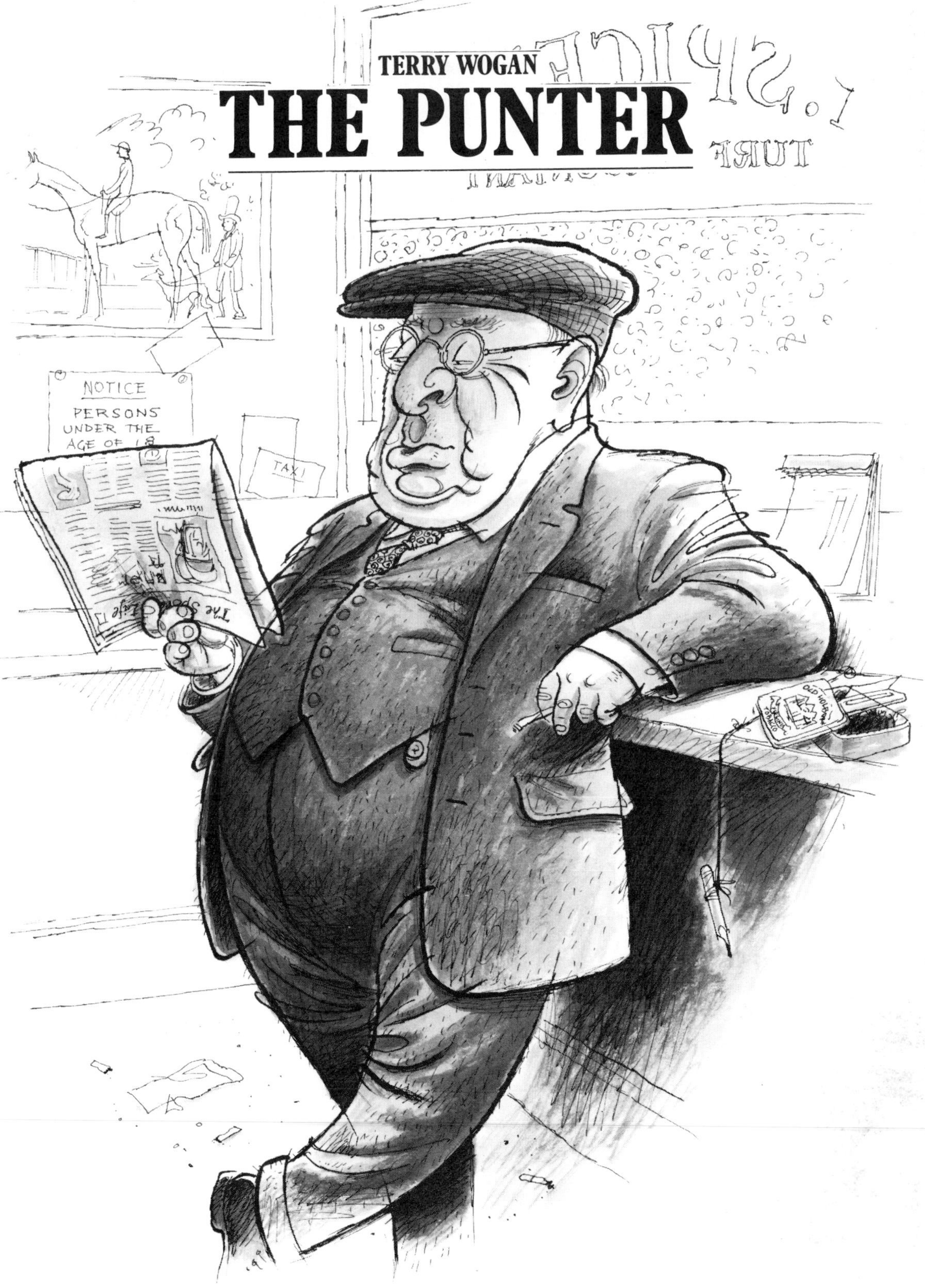

TO HORSE! TO HORSE!

The punter is of average height. Middle-aged, but of a cheery, optimistic countenance that belies his years. The optimism in his sparkling eyes is often confused with child-like innocence, and rightly so. This Elysian innocence derives from a Micawberish belief that something is sure to turn up, viz, a winner. Today's the Day. The Big One. The Daughter's Wedding. The Wife's Fun Fur. Two Fingers to the Boss. Winter In The Bahamas. Ascot In A Topper. Begone Dull Care . . .

The punter is a dreamer, a romantic who places his trust in Newsboy, The Scout, Robin Goodfellow, Peter O'Sullevan, *The Sporting Chronicle*, *The Sporting Life*, and someone who Hears It Hot From The Very Lips Of A Newmarket Stable Lad. It never occurs to him to question why, if all these redoubtable seers know so much, *they're* not wintering in the Bahamas, or indeed buying the place.

The punter's eyes are somewhat crossed from the avid perusal of all this inside information, and his left ear is larger than his right from so much listening to stable gossip. He is a veritable mine of maxims. 'Better,' he will intone, 'the short-priced winner than the long-priced loser.' His nose has a marked list to starboard, from incessant tapping with a knowledgeable index-finger while delivering such sage gems as: 'He's not making *that* journey for the good of his health!' This pithy *bon mot* is usually evoked when the punter notices that a horse trained in Yorkshire is down to run at Devon and Exeter, probably because the trainer wants to visit his grandmother in Torquay!

The punter is steeped in racing parlance, and his conversation, delivered *sotto voce* from the corner of his mobile mouth, is liberally sprinkled with references to 'trappy' handicaps, horses 'running green', winners 'on the bit', and losers that 'did not trouble the judge'.

Of all the racing confraternity, only the punter wears a cap, usually pushed back on the cranium, the better to scratch his head in bewilderment as yet another certainty bites the dust. His outer garment is a raincoat, its pockets stuffed to bursting with little bits of paper covered in arcane hieroglyphs denoting cross-trebles, yankees and the ITV Seven.

Just as there are no bad drivers, lousy lovers or people who can't hold their drink, there is no such thing as a Losing Punter. The worst he ever does is 'break even'. Which may explain the number of poverty-stricken bookies you see around these days . . . .

The British punter is probably the best-informed in the world. Newspapers, radio, television and specialist publications such as those produced by the admirable Timeform Organization, combine to provide a fund of knowledge that should keep him, if not one jump ahead of the bookie, at least in with an equal chance. Unfortunately, of course, the bookmaker has the same reading list, and tends to be rather better than the punter in his interpretation of it.

However, even the keenest student of the form book will need a little luck, for the glorious uncertainty of racing is its very fascination, and the first lesson any punter must learn is that there is no such thing as a racing certainty. A horse is not a machine, and however magnificent, sleek, powerful and fit it may appear, a nagging tooth, a stomach ache or a minor muscular discomfort can make all the difference between winning and losing. So, too, can a wrong decision, taken in a split-second, by even the most skilful jockey, while a mistake by another horse in the race can kibosh the chances of the most worthy favourite.

But such is the confidence of so many punters that thoughts of this kind are of no consequence. Visit any betting shop and listen. Before the race you will quickly identify the self-appointed form expert. With all the bravado in the world he will announce his selection after a cursory glance at the newspaper pinned on the wall. If it happened to have been beaten on its last outing he will tell anyone prepared to listen that it wasn't 'off' that day. If it had won, then clearly it is the horse in form.

Comparative form with the other horses in the race is not something he is likely to dwell upon, let alone understand, and the chances are that he will also let you know, very confidentially, that he had a good tip for it from a friend who is very friendly indeed with the trainer's secretary.

He then places his bet, leans back against the wall, nonchalantly rolls a cigarette and feigns a total indifference to the early part of the race commentary. He is, after all, only waiting for the 'weighed in' so that he can collect the money. As the race develops, his air of confidence will increase if the 'good thing' is reported up with the leaders. A slight nervous twitch will become apparent if the commentator fails to mention it. Should the horse win, he will qualify immediately as Bore of the Year with repeated cries of 'It was obvious, wasn't it', interspersed with 'I told you so' and 'It's like taking candy from a baby'. Should *you* have failed to take his advice, you would do well at this point to slip away quickly before your stupidity is broadcast to everyone in the shop.

The chances are, however, that you will not be forced out, and instead will be able to listen to a vitriolic explanation of why he has just been robbed. Of one thing you can be certain: that explanation will not include any admission of miscalculation on his part. The fault will lie entirely with the jockey ('I always knew he was a crook'), the trainer ('What a bastard that man is'), the judge ('He couldn't tell if it was raining'), or the stewards ('They must have been in on it too'). If his bet exceeded a fiver it is likely that the blame will be shared between all these double-dyed villains who conspired to do him out of his money.

In fact, racing in Britain is probably straighter than anywhere in the world, though the prospect of easy, tax-free money has in the past attracted, and always will attract, undesirable elements. Occasionally they will succeed in their less-than-honest endeavours, though today both the authorities and the bookmakers are well equipped with the most modern communications and technology with which to protect the integrity of the sport.

Today it would be impossible, for example, to repeat the audacious theft perpetrated in 1898 on the bookmakers, who paid out fortunes on the result of an entirely fictitious race-meeting. At that time there were many more little racecourses up and down the country, and when *The Sportsman* received a list of runners, their weights and other details from the Clerk of the Course at 'Trodmore', a Mr G. Martin, and a request for them to be published before the 'forthcoming meeting', the paper did so without question. Came the big day, the bookies took some hefty bets on Reaper to win the Handicap Hurdle, together with a

THE PUNTER

variety of doubles and trebles.

The following morning *The Sportsman* published the Trodmore results, supplied by Mr Martin, and sure enough Reaper had won at the rewarding odds of 5–1. Many, but not all, of the doubles and trebles added to the bookmakers' liabilities.

Some bookmakers paid out immediately, others asked *The Sporting Life* to confirm the results. This it did – by copying out the winners and their prices from *The Sportsman*! Unfortunately a printing error changed Reaper's price from 5–1 to 5–2, and to clear up the resulting confusion a letter was sent to Mr Martin. When this was returned 'not known', the plot was uncovered, but not before a large part of the 'winnings' had been collected.

More recently, a clever conspiracy to defraud the bookmakers was proved in court after an Irish owner and a Scottish trainer had sought to land a £300,000 coup with a horse called Gay Future. The basis of the plot was simple enough – to bring a useful horse from Ireland to run in a very modest race at a little Bank Holiday meeting at Cartmel in the Lake District. It was to be backed in London, knowing that the money could not be sent back to the course to shorten the price. All perfectly honest. Unfortunately the plot thickened as the plans were laid, and the horse that arrived in the Scottish trainer's yard a month or so before the race, purporting to be Gay Future, was a useless creature. The real Gay Future remained in training in Ireland until two days before the coup when he

was sent over and the substitution made. Then, in order to allay any bookmakers' suspicions, many of the wagers were made as doubles and trebles with two useless horses from the same stable – real mug punters' bets which are meat and drink to the bookies. However, the plan was to withdraw the other two horses at the last minute, so that the doubles and trebles would be treated as single bets on Gay Future.

Further embellishment was given to the plot by rubbing soapflakes on Gay Future's legs before he got into the parade ring, making him appear to be in a lather, and

therefore an unattractive betting proposition to punters on the course. The London bookmakers' intelligence system detected the flood of money for Gay Future four hours before the race, and although they stopped taking bets on the horse when only about £5,000 of the intended £30,000 was staked, they were unable to get any of the money back to remote little Cartmel in order to shorten the price. Gay Future duly won at 10 – 1, and about £15,000 was collected before the big bookmakers announced they were refusing to pay out pending investigations by the Serious Crime Squad of Scotland Yard. Eventually the story unfolded, prosecutions followed, the owner and trainer were fined, all bets declared void, and the Jockey Club delivered the *coup de grâce* by banning both men from racecourses for ten years.

Such stories attract much publicity and confirm the popular misconception that the whole game is crooked. They do, however, serve one useful purpose, for while there is suspicion that all may not be strictly above-board, our self-appointed expert in the betting shop can put all his miscalculations down to villainy. Were it otherwise, and the sport proved whiter than white, he would have no-one to blame but himself.

For the vast majority of punters, their daily dabble is nothing more than a harmless recreational pursuit bringing a little colour and excitement into their lives. The shrewd ones will acknowledge that to stand any chance of winning they must understand the form, appreciate the subtleties of weight, distance,

time and going, be highly selective in their betting, and, above all, look for value in the prices they take. Horseracing is fun. Betting on it regularly, to be profitable, is hard work.

One of horseracing's great raconteurs is Lord Willoughby de Broke, a lifelong lover of the sport, an ex-steward of the Jockey Club, and an enthusiastic if not always successful punter. Not for nothing did the Crazy Gang acknowledge his presence in the Victoria Palace audience as 'Lord Willoughby de Skint'.

Lord Willoughby recalls a disastrous meeting on York's lovely Knavesmire course between the wars,

TERRY WOGAN
THE BOOKIE

TO HORSE! TO HORSE!

The bookie is much maligned. No-one in British racing is more misunderstood, more vilified. Yet this remarkable character continues to serve the ungrateful British Public, surviving, it sometimes seems, by sheer moral fortitude alone.

He is a man of no more than average height, and wears the regulation brown hat like any other self-respecting racegoer. He scorns the soup-stained grey-green raincoat of the pathetic punter, and favours his sturdy sheepskin, the better to withstand the biting blizzards of Fakenham, the soaking rains of Yarmouth, the slings and arrows of outrageous fortune-hunters.

The bookie is one of Nature's gentlemen. Soft-spoken, with kindly eyes that twinkle from behind bookish horn-rimmed spectacles. He is a self-made man, but with none of the ostentatious show, the noisy assertiveness of that breed. He is a family man, whose job takes him away too far, too often, from his beloved hearth and home. His wife, a quiet woman in an understated mink jacket and barely discernible diamond earrings, is ever in the background, his helpmeet, his strong support. His children go to public school, and from there to the army or the priesthood.

Indeed, the bookie's calling is akin to the priesthood. Lonely, ascetic, steeped in the mystic rites of tic-tac, and arcane calculation. He is a keeper of men's souls, an upholder of the moral law. Particularly the one about the payment of debts. Stoical in the face of loss or gain, he

epitomizes Kipling's ideal of treating those two imposters, Triumph or Disaster, just the same. Indeed he can often be seen to laugh openly at Disaster, particularly if he has managed to 'lay-off' with some other kindly fellow-bookie eager to lighten his load.

The bookie is a poor man. He is not, as he often admonishes his

flock, 'made of money'. Heaven knows, he tries his all to give the best possible odds to the clamorous punter but, try as he may, he cannot be unfair, bound as he is by the sacred trust he shares with his fellow accountants of the Turf. By the time a rapacious government has taken its

THE BOOKIE

gruelling toll, and he has paid, out of the goodness of his heart, ridiculous odds to the punters, there is little left for the bookie himself.

Why, then, does he do it? Why expose himself to privation and hardship, to the screeches and protests of the ugly mob? Who is he doing it for? What does he hope to gain? Well, as we have already seen, gain or profit hardly comes into it, because it *has* to be done, because it's there, because a man's got to do what a man's got to do. And he's doing it for you and for me, that's who. God knows, it's not for himself.

At the end of the day as the weary bookmaker slips between the welcoming sheets, his wife, 'the little woman', will say: 'Have a good day, dear?'

'Oh, you know, not bad. . . .'

'Lost more money, did you?'

'Ah well, the punters have to live too, you know.'

'They just don't appreciate you, dear.'

'No, they'll never understand . . . but they *need* me. . . . Good night, dear.'

'Good night, Willie.'

TONY FAIRBAIRN

Most bookmakers have mothers, in whom they take a kindly interest. Some also treat dogs and other dumb animals pretty well, extending such consideration even to punters, on occasion. Few bookmakers, however, actually wear the traditional uniform of loud check suits and brown bowler hats, and virtually none is agile enough to do a bunk on the rare occasions when his liabilities exceed the contents of his satchel.

All of them, however, have to live with the popular image of their calling, a handicap of such magnitude that in seeking to overcome it they tend towards projecting an unconvincing air of sanctity, which is worse.

The truth of the matter is that the British love their bookies. They are 'the old enemy' with whom every punter wages an affectionate, never-ending war, but whose prospects of success in an extended campaign are as remote as Ronnie Corbett's chance of winning an Olympic medal for the ladies' shot-putt.

But no matter. The bookmakers of Britain provide a service which is unmatched by any country in the world. The variety of bets available, the opportunity to wager right up to the off in a betting shop hundreds of miles away from

71

the course, speedy payouts, and a personal rapport with the Honest Joe concerned are treasured privileges of the British punter. And long may it last.

Sadly, however, the traditional Honest Joes are a dying breed. Every year more and more of them take early retirement by selling their businesses to the big multiple bookmakers, public companies controlled more by accountants and efficiency experts than by the gambling bookmakers of old. However, it must be said that bookmakers' profitability is by no means as excessive as is generally thought, and the margins today are much smaller than they were in the early days of betting shops when John Banks, the extrovert Scottish bookie, described them as a licence to print money.

The skill required in 'making a book' is considerable. Ideally the bookmaker will seek to attract bets on every horse in a race so that whatever wins he will have to pay out in winnings about £77 for every £100 he has taken in stakes. The avaricious government takes £8 out of every hundred – a wickedly high rate when it is considered that betting money is turned over again and again, so that the true rate of taxation on the money *spent*, that is, lost, by punters each year is nearer 50 per cent. Rather less than £1 in every hundred goes back to help finance the sport itself through the Horserace Betting Levy Board, and the remaining £14 is the bookmaker's gross profit. Most of that is swallowed up in rent, rates, staff and other costs leaving him, if he is

lucky, with about two or three per cent net profit.

But while the off-course bookmaker is rapidly becoming a super-efficient if impersonal cog in the wheel of big business, the on-

THE BOOKIE

course bookie who day after day travels from racecourse to racecourse, come hail or come shine, remains as colourful an individual as ever. It is upon him that the whole structure of betting is based, for it is the betting market on the course which determines the odds at which bets are settled in the 12,000 or so shops throughout the country.

In 1981 the bookmakers' betting turnover on horse racing reached £2,600 million – but before the critics make moral judgments on such profligate expenditure the distinction must be drawn clearly between turnover and what the punters actually spend.

If ten men go to a bookie, each with £10 in his pocket, the most they can *spend* between them is £100. But during the course of six races they are likely to *turn over* about £270 if the money they win is reinvested each time, assuming that the normal rate of winning and losing is maintained. And so it is that the national betting *turnover* of £2,600 million represents an actual *expenditure* of about £500 million, which compares with £5,655 million spent on beer and £5,528 million on baccy.

Indeed, any international league table demonstrating the betting habits of various countries would show the British well behind the punters of countries like Australia, Hong Kong and Japan, all of which would give nightmares and a permanent twitch to the Churches' Council on Gambling. That august body, as mentioned earlier, issued a weighty report some years ago which exonerated the BBC for allowing

Wogan's Winner to be broadcast each morning. It was, their reverences maintained, a real disincentive to bet, so rarely did it win! Their timing, however, was bad, for it followed three successive seasons in which

Wogan's Wager actually showed a profit. And in the last of these the profit was ten per cent greater than that shown by Robin Goodfellow of the *Daily Mail* who won the £1,000 prize awarded by *The Sporting Life* to the most successful tipster in their daily Naps Table.

It was in that same season that the William Hill Organization recorded one of the most remarkable betting stories connected with Wogan's Winner. A man walked into Hill House in London, tipped

TO HORSE! TO HORSE!

£20,000 out of a suitcase and asked for it to be put on Wogan's Winner.

'And what was that this morning?' asked the bewildered manager. 'I don't know,' replied the punter, 'but I expect the BBC will tell you if you ring them up.'

Hill's got the answer and took the bet. It won at 5–2, and after paying tax at the then relatively modest rate of six per cent, the man was £45,800 richer. Asking to be paid in cash, he returned the next day for his money. Before leaving, he put £25,000 on the table and again asked for it to be placed on Wogan's Winner, without knowing what it was. That won also, at 2–1, making him another £45,500.

The same procedure followed on the third day when £40,000 was placed on yet another triumph for the Racing Bulletin – a 9–2 winner, earning the intrepid punter a further £166,800 and bringing his total on three days to more than a quarter of a million pounds.

No-one at Hill's discovered the name of the man, and he never went back to Hill House again. Nor did the Racing Bulletin Team get so much as a postcard from his tropical hideaway to thank them for their part in this extraordinary affair.

TONY FAIRBAIRN
MAKING
A BETTER BET

TO HORSE! TO HORSE!

Volumes have been written about the science and skills of backing racehorses and it would be foolish to think that this single chapter will put you on the road to riches. But there are six basic rules which might help keep the wolf from the door a little longer. Two *don'ts*, two *nevers* and two *always*.

Don't try and back a horse in every race. It is the quick way to the poorhouse. *Don't* chase your losses on the basis that sooner or later you're bound to win. That is an even quicker route. *Never* stake more than you can afford to lose, for, sure as hell, you will. *Never* back a horse only because it lost last time you backed it; it probably will again. *Always* look for value in betting. The odds quoted by the bookmaker for each horse may reflect the volume of betting more than the respective chances of the individual horse, and a hot favourite can often mean better value may be had with another runner in the race. Nonetheless the old adage about a short-priced winner being a great deal better than a long-priced loser should never be forgotten. Finally, *always* remember that the best tipster is the form book. It won't provide every winner, but it will do a great deal better than granny's hat pin.

And so, with these words of wisdom ringing in your ears, a sporting paper under your arm and a pair of binoculars over your shoulder, away with you to Ayr or Ascot, Carlisle or Cheltenham, York or Yarmouth or, indeed, any one of the other 54 courses. All will offer you a warm welcome and a fun day.

On arrival you will be faced with a choice of enclosures: the Members or Club, Tattersalls or Grandstand and Paddock, the Silver Ring and, in many cases, a course enclosure in the infield. As with anything else, you get what you pay for, and the facilities – much improved on most courses over the past twenty years – will vary according to the price of admission. This ranges from about £15 in Members for the big prestige meetings to less than £1 for the cheaper enclosures on an ordinary day. But unless you are feeling very skint, either the Club or Tattersalls enclosures offer the best value, for it is here that you will be able to watch the horses in the parade ring before each race, and see the winner and placed horses unsaddled afterwards. Tattersalls is also the main betting ring.

Ideally, you will have studied the form in advance, but before having a bet go and look at the horses in the paddock. The subtleties of conformation probably escape even the most avid racegoer, but with just a little experience it is readily apparent when a horse is well: it has a spring in its step, it is 'on its toes', and has a sleek and shiny coat covering a well-muscled lean frame, an alert and watchful eye. The owners, trainers and jockeys will assemble in the parade ring while the horses circle around, and although it is not generally regarded as being a great pointer, actor Robert Morley has a theory which he claims can be profitable to the keen observer at this stage in the proceedings. Disregard, he says, those horses whose owners turn up with their wives and families. Concentrate instead on the owner who has brought with him a beautiful dolly-bird he is obviously seeking to impress. His is the horse which will be doing its best!

Study of form, study of horse, and study of owners' girl-friends completed, the time has come to make the bet. This can be done with a bookmaker or on the Tote. The bookmaker offers odds against each horse and the punter can either take the price quoted at the time the bet is made, or the 'starting price' which is the price available at the 'off'.

Look at several bookmakers' boards before making the bet, particularly if your selection is not one of the first two or three in the betting. Prices can vary from one to another, and, in the North of England and Scotland in particular, it is not unusual to see the longer-priced horses vary by as much as six to ten points. If you back the winner at 10–1 it can be galling to find that, had you walked an extra few yards, you could have had 16–1.

Tattersalls' bookmakers don't take 10p bets. Most of them get pretty shirty about 50p, too, but there is usually a racecourse betting shop which will be happy to take the small wagers. However, if you are going to splurge a couple of pounds, decide exactly what you want to do, and with the cash in your hand walk up to the bookmaker of your choice and say loud and clear: 'I would like two pounds to win on So-and-so' at whatever price he is quoting at the time. If So-and-so happens to be 5–1, you could hand him £2 and say: 'I would like ten pounds to two, So-and-so.' Either way he will take your money, call the bet to his clerk who will enter it in the book, and hand you a numbered ticket. Don't lose it – you might have backed a winner!

If you have, you will need to return to the bookmaker after the 'weighed-in' is announced on the public address system, hand him the ticket and claim £12 – the £10 you have won plus your £2 stake – less tax, which on the racecourse is at the relatively tolerable rate of 4 per cent. This is payable on winnings *and* stakes, so the Chancellor will nick 48p of your windfall.

Betting with the Tote is a rather more orderly affair requiring no mathematical skill. The Tote

TO HORSE! TO HORSE!

operates 'pool betting', so that all the money staked in a race goes into the pool; after a deduction for overheads and tax, this is divided among the winners in proportion to their stake. The Tote Dividends are declared to a 10p stake, and announced after the race.

Each-way betting, on the first, second and third horses to finish, is possible with both the bookies and the Tote, but unless you fancy a longshot it is seldom worthwhile. Bookmakers offer only one-fifth the quoted odds for 'a place' in races with more than eight runners. In handicaps with more than twelve runners they pay a quarter the odds, and with sixteen or more runners in a handicap they pay also on fourth place.

With the Tote the 'place' pool operates in much the same way as the win pool but the dividends are unpredictable. A long-priced horse can sometimes return a miserable dividend, whereas a third or fourth favourite may give its supporters a welcome surprise.

As with all Totalisator betting, one large, successful bet can play havoc with the dividends, while one large, unsuccessful bet can provide an unexpected bonanza for those backing the other horses. Some years ago, the Sheikh of Abu Dhabi made a State Visit to Britain, and for relaxation chose to attend a Saturday afternoon meeting at Windsor. The Sheikh, at that time reputedly the richest man in the world with an income of several million pounds daily, occupied the Royal Box and was invited down to the Parade Ring to see at close quarters the horses

engaged in the big race of the day. John Rickman was covering the racing for ITV and reckoned that the viewers would be interested to learn of the Sheikh's selection. The Sheikh's approval for this idea was sought, and given readily, for the Sheikh, like so many Arabs, believed he had a pretty good eye for a horse. My job was to escort him and convey his choice to John Rickman, who would then broadcast it to the nation.

It was a big field with more than twenty runners, and after careful deliberation the Sheikh settled upon some particularly undistinguished animal who, it must be said, looked more like a hat-rack than a racehorse. Nevertheless, this was his choice, proving perhaps that every eye sees its own beauty. I reported to Gentleman John as arranged, learning from him that the

MAKING A BETTER BET

State Visitor had picked a 25–1 chance. On returning to the Paddock the Sheikh's interpreter advised me that His Excellency wished to have a bet on the horse and asked me to arrange it.

Something approaching sheer panic set in. After all, if this man was to invest just one-hundredth of his day's pay on this wretched beast, it would knock the shaky on-course betting market for six. Indeed, it would be doubtful if I could get on one-thousandth of His Excellency's daily income!

Then I thought of the Tote. This would take whatever the Sheikh wanted to invest. If he was successful – which seemed highly improbable – he would receive the minimum

dividend of 4s 2d for every four shillings he staked. If he lost, as seemed certain, the winner would return a massive dividend because of the unexpectedly huge pool. As all this flashed through my mind an excitable conversation was continuing in Arabic, and the Sheikh eventually nodded towards a huge white-robed attendant who turned out to be the Keeper of the Oily Purse. Instructions were issued, and from the depths of his flowing garment the Oily Purse was produced, and from it extracted a crisp new ten shilling note – 50p to younger readers. This was handed over with great solemnity in the middle of Windsor's attractive paddock, and I was left to negotiate the best deal possible. In betting parlance, I 'stuck' the bet, pocketed the cash and accepted the risk. The horse duly finished last, and I have the ten bob note to this day.

But I still sometimes ponder on what might have happened to that Tote Pool if I had been asked to put £100,000 or so on a hopeless outsider. I'm sorry, too, because with that sort of money in the Pool it would have been well worthwhile putting a tenner on every other runner in the race!

Most newcomers to racing are unlikely to get involved in the more complex bets which prove a great attraction to so many punters looking for a big return on a relatively small stake. On the Tote there is a *Forecast Pool* where punters must select first and second in either order. There is also the *Daily Double*, usually on the third and fifth races, in which the punter has to find both winners, and the *Tote Daily Treble* where he is looking for all three winners. The *Tote Jackpot*, in which racegoers are asked to find the winners of the first six races, can pay huge dividends because when, as frequently happens, no-one wins, the pool is carried forward to another meeting, and builds up to provide a huge prize.

Betting shops, both on and off course, thrive on a whole series of complicated bets. Doubles, trebles and accumulators are straightforward enough. One stake only is required and the winnings plus the stake from the first selection all go on to the second (a double), which all goes on to the third (a treble), the fourth, fifth and so on, according to the number of horses chosen in different races. It's the fast way to a fortune – always provided, of course, that you pick only winners. When one gets beaten, the bet is lost.

More complicated are the multiple bets. A *Patent* involves selecting three horses in different races, backing each of them singly, and coupling them in three doubles and a treble. Seven bets are involved and one winner will mean that you have something to come back. It can be profitable too. A £1 Patent will cost £7, but if all those selected win at 3–1 you will collect £12 for the three singles bets, £48 for the three doubles, and £64 for the treble, a total of £124. It is better still with one good-priced winner, say at 10–1, and a couple of 2–1 chances. That would return £191. But in most betting shops you will have to forfeit ten per cent in deductions for tax and bookmakers' overheads.

A *Yankee* is four selections coupled in eleven bets, six doubles, four trebles and one accumulator, and you will need at least two winners before claiming anything back. A *Super Yankee* is the same sort of wager, involving 26 bets on five selections. *Up and Down* is a single stake on each of two horses. Anything to come from either goes back on to the other. A *Trixie* is like a Patent but without the single bets, while a *Heinz* is, not surprisingly, a bet with 57 possible winning combinations over six horses – 15 doubles, 20 trebles, 15 four-horse accumulators, six five-timers and one six-horse accumulator. Great if you win – expensive if you don't! There are *Dundee Shuffles*, *Fidos*, *Union Jacks*, *Yaps*, *Round Robins*, *Round the Clocks*, *Roundabouts*, *Rounders*, and even a *Goliath* – 247 bets coupling eight selections in doubles, trebles, and every possible sort of accumulator, but these are for the seasoned punter who is both a supreme optimist and a likely candidate for the Flat Earth Society.

The odd double, treble, Patent and Yankee can be fun bets and occasionally profitable, but remember that bookmakers love to take these multiple bets. Their usual profit margin is multiplied five or six fold. Nuff said?

TO HORSE! TO HORSE!

With the exception of Sir Gordon Richards, who is an honorary member, there are no jockeys or ex-jockeys in the Jockey Club. Nor, apart from about thirty-five days a year when racing or the Sales take place at Newmarket, does the Club open its imposing doors to allow members to enjoy the elegant facilities. It is, however, the ruling body of racing, and has been for a couple of hundred years. As such it grants the licences to jockeys, trainers and officials, it makes the Rules of Racing, controls the fixture list and race programmes, and imposes the discipline.

While it is a source of irritation to its critics that Eton and the Brigade of Guards tend to provide a disproportionate number of its members, anyone, from whatever background, elected to the Jockey Club today is expected to share in its administrative functions and not simply enjoy the privileges associated with it. Nor is it any longer totally male-dominated, for the Sex Discrimination Act, a certain amount of outside pressure, and the emergence of a number of ladies with outstanding racing knowledge and ability led inevitably to their inclusion in the hierarchy of the Sport, consequent adjustments to the plumbing in the Club rooms, and the odd case of apoplexy among the more reactionary members.

Like any supreme authority the Jockey Club is no stranger to criticism, but while almost every faction in racing will complain about some aspect of the Club's policy or legislation, few of them would fail to endorse the basic principle that 'Jockey Club Rules – O K!'

Indeed, in recent years, all sorts of investigations and inquiries have been held to seek ways of bringing about a more democratic form of government in racing, but none of the alterations proposed, most of them based on some form of expensive bureaucracy, has bettered the present system which is dependent upon voluntary service, impartiality and integrity.

When the Jockey Club was founded – or, more probably, just happened – in the middle of the 18th century, it had no ambition to control anything. 'Jockey' at that time meant simply 'horseman', so the Club was just a small association of men who met to arrange 'matches' between their horses, and wager on the outcome. This they did at the Star and Garter Coffee House in London, and it wasn't until their headquarters moved to another coffee house, this time in Newmarket High Street, that they began to have any real influence on the sport.

The Newmarket Coffee House adopted by the Jockey Club in those days still stands, virtually unchanged, an historic room incorporated into the modern buildings which house the Club today. Just who those first members were, no-one quite knows, but clearly they wielded considerable power over the way racing was conducted on the Heath, and it was not long before the 'Newmarket Rules' they drew up became a blueprint for racing everywhere else in Britain. Such was their influence that other courses began to refer their own disputes to Newmarket for adjudication, and so frequently were they called upon to act as arbitrators that they would do so only when the courses involved raced under Newmarket Rules.

So it was that the authority of the Jockey Club was born, and it is a measure of that authority that it remained virtually unchallenged despite any legal basis for well over two hundred years, a situation which changed in 1971 when it was granted the Royal Charter under which it operates today.

During those years it was well served by men like Lord George Bentinck and Admiral Rous, great reformers of racing, who imposed a discipline on the Turf that was stern, often harsh, but applied without fear or favour to kings and commoners, so that those 'warned off' Newmarket Heath stayed warned off – not only there but from every other racecourse as well.

Not that such pillars of the turf as Lord George Bentinck were beyond the perpetration of a substantial gambling coup or two. In 1836 Lord George owned Elis, the strongly fancied ante-post favourite for the St Leger. In those days horses would travel from course to course the hard way, and Elis had a 250-mile walk ahead of him from his stable at Goodwood to Doncaster. When the bookmakers discovered a week before the big race that Elis had not left Sussex, they assumed he was an unlikely runner, and, anxious to take as much money as they could from mug punters who did not share this information, they pushed out his price to tempting and apparently very generous odds. At this point Lord George stepped in with a series of massive wagers, for he and his estate carpenter alone knew that they had just constructed the first horsebox and could get Elis to Doncaster in three days, pulled by teams of horses. Elis duly won, Lord George collected a small fortune, and the Jockey Club preserves to this day in its Newmarket home a wheel of that first horsebox.

Betting is no longer any sort of preoccupation for the members of the Jockey Club. Indeed, despite the fact that there are one or two fearless punters left within the membership, it is a source of concern to bookmakers that the Club does not give greater consideration to the needs of the betting industry when arranging the racing programmes. But while the Jockey Club has gone some way down this path it resists the pressures which would allow betting to dominate the administration of the sport, despite the reliance of racing on a tiny share of the betting turnover.

Membership of the Jockey Club, which now incorporates the old National Hunt Committee which controlled steeplechasing and hurdle racing when the Jockey Club was concerned only with flat racing, is limited to about a hundred. Of these, seven are elected to serve as Stewards, the inner cabinet who control the day-to-day running of the sport. Apart from the Senior Steward and his deputy, each Steward has responsibility for a particular department – licensing, discipline, race programming, finance, or racecourses. Each is aided by a small committee from within the general membership, and a highly professional team from Weatherbys, racing's civil servants, and needs to spend several days a week fulfilling his responsibilities.

The Stewards are, of course, unpaid, and their only reward lies in satisfaction from their achievements. Not surprisingly, perhaps, the number of people with the necessary knowledge and time available is limited, and the fact that they are drawn largely from among the wealthy racehorse owners leads to charges of élitism, and not infrequent demands that the membership base of the Jockey Club be broadened to include a more representative element from the grass roots of the sport.

Whether the grass roots, the professionals, could provide men or women with sufficient time to spend on the many, varied and complex problems of administration is debatable. Equally debatable would be their objectivity, for in an industry with so many sectional interests there is little room at the top for those pursuing self-interest at the expense of the sport as a whole. Indeed it has been suggested that when some slight broadening of the base took place a few years ago it introduced into the Club a tiny but influential element more concerned with the preservation of top-class racing, through the increase in prize money for the best flat races, than in maintaining the run-of-the-mill sport which day in and day out occupies the majority of owners, trainers, jockeys and racecourses, and, of course, keeps the multi-million pound betting industry ticking over.

Although by no means the largest part of its work, the disciplinary responsibilities of the Club attract most attention. Minor misdemeanours which infringe the Rules of Racing are dealt with on a daily basis by the Stewards of Meetings who may or may not be members of the Jockey Club itself. More serious cases are dealt with by the Disciplinary Committee of the Jockey Club, a formidable judicial body whose word can be, but rarely is, challenged only in the High Court. Legal representation is now a feature of these hearings, but because they take place behind closed doors, they are not infrequently, but unjustly, referred to as Kangaroo Courts or Star Chambers. They can, however, control the destiny of trainers and jockeys so that no-one called before them to explain a breach of the Rules is likely to sleep soundly the night before their appearance.

To some extent the fear engendered by a summons to Portman Square – the Jockey Club's London headquarters – is a hangover from the days of rougher justice when indefinite suspensions were imposed, when 'warning off' was for life and meant the end of a jockey's or trainer's career. Today sentences are meted out in strict accordance with the laws of natural justice, and the evidence called is of the highest technical standard, be it that of camera patrol film in the case of a riding offence, or of highly qualified chemists in doping cases. And penalties involving the suspension of a jockey's or trainer's licence are for stated periods, generally measured in weeks or months rather than years. Not that the ultimate sentence of permanent banishment cannot be imposed in cases of the direst villainy.

Because the financial rewards are potentially great, racing will always attract those who aren't too fussy about sticking strictly to the Rules, but racing in Britain is as straight as anywhere in the world as a result of the ceaseless vigilance of the authorities.

Recent years have found the Jockey Club involved much more deeply in aspects of racing which previously it regarded as outside its administrative function. Largely because the sport has become an industry in the space of a quarter of a century, the Club has had to develop a political lobby, make legislative

provision for the terms and conditions of the labour force, study the financial implications of its fixture-list and race-programming, give greater heed to medical arrangements and safety standards, and act where possible in accordance

with the needs of the paying public. It's a far cry from those early days at Newmarket where races were run on a variety of courses during an afternoon, so that only the mounted gentry could get from one to another, and the lower orders of society could be prevented from following!

Knowledge and understanding of racing affairs is still not always matched in the Club by an appreciation of life as most of us live it. A very senior member, a peer of the realm, a man of immense charm with a lifetime of public service behind him, and a great lover of the Turf, came to see me some years ago, troubled by the effect televised racing could have on racecourse attendances.

'I watched television last Saturday,' he said. 'Frightfully good y'know.'

I murmured agreement. After all, had not both channels been televising racing regularly for a decade or more and become highly skilled in the art?

'No,' he said. 'I mean awfully good!' Again I nodded agreement.

'It seemed to me,' he went on, 'as I watched Peter O'Sullevan last Saturday, that I couldn't be the only one, and that around the country there were thousands and thousands of people sitting in their council houses, drinking their port and watching the racing!'

MONEY, MONEY, MONEY...

TO HORSE! TO HORSE!

The Jockey Club imposes the rules and governs the sport. It does not, however, control the purse-strings of the industry which is financed from other sources – by racehorse owners, racecourses, and the Horserace Betting Levy Board.

It is the owners who provide the horses, pay the training bills, the travelling costs of the horses, and the jockeys. In addition they have to pay entry fees which contribute significantly towards the prize money for each race; of almost £20 million won in 1981, more than £5 million came from owners in entry fees. Owners also pay heavily towards the Jockey Club's administrative costs, a burden they share with the racecourses. In all, the owners put about £70 million into the sport each year, quite apart from the £15 million or so they spend on buying horses, few of which will keep their value let alone show a profit.

Racecourses, too, have a huge capital investment in the sport. There are 60 of them altogether, ranging from the northernmost, Perth, to Newton Abbot in the South-West. Many of them have grandstands which have cost millions to build – or would certainly cost millions to replace – and these, coupled with ever-increasing land values, put racecourse investment in the sport in the region of £250 million. Return on this is pitifully small, and as it is doubtful if the combined profitability of all 60 courses exceeds £1 million a year the moral is: don't buy shares in a racecourse!

Racecourses also provide about £5½ million in prize money

each year, almost £3 million from their own resources, and another £2.6 million from the sponsors they attract. They pay nearly £1½ million towards the costs of the Jockey Club, and, with help from the Levy Board, they carry the risks of abandonment for snow, ice, rain, and, occasionally,

MONEY, MONEY, MONEY...

too much sun. Their income is limited to the £12 million or so they get through the turnstiles each year, £1 million from television fees, £1.3 million for the commentary relayed from the courses to the betting shops, various grants from the Levy Board, and anything they can get for letting the car parks as caravan sites on non-racing days, or the grandstands for exhibitions or dog shows.

The Levy Board, now under the Chairmanship of Sir Ian Trethowan (whose Foreword to this book resulted from shameless crawling by the authors), provides the balance of the money needed to keep the game afloat. The income of the Board results from a levy of fractionally less than one penny in every pound of bookmakers' turnover plus a contribution from the Tote. This produces about £21 million, a lifeline without which the sport would be in dire straits and totally incapable of providing the volume of racing necessary to keep the betting industry operational six days a week.

An Act of Parliament was required to establish the Horserace Betting Levy Board, and to empower it to raise money from betting. Furthermore, the Board is responsible to the Home Secretary for the collection and distribution of what is, in effect, money raised by the sport for the sport. But because it is 'public money', it is often regarded as a subsidy. This can lead to controversy when it is suggested that the levy is taken from the punters, many of whom are at the less-privileged end of society, and given as prize money to the owners, most,

but by no means all of whom are at the richer end of the scale. However, this emotive Robin Hood-in-reverse concept owes more to political dogmatism than logic, since it is hardly inappropriate for those who enjoy a flutter to contribute towards the sport which provides their enjoyment, particularly as the levy was introduced primarily to compensate racing for lost turnstile revenue when off-course betting was legalized in the early Sixties.

There is misconception too, in the view that the existing levy is hopelessly inadequate to meet the needs of the sport, for while it could be doubled or trebled and still fail to meet all the bills, there is little justification for maintaining that a substantially greater portion of the costs incurred by, say, the owners, should be borne by the punters. The truth of the matter is that no-one is forced into buying a racehorse, nor is anyone forced into having a bet, and while the owner and the punter are largely interdependent, the balance of that interdependence is finely tuned. It would be as financially disastrous to double the levy as it would be to abolish it, for plundering the pockets of the punters simply reduces betting turnover, as the Chancellor of the Exchequer has found to his cost, while reducing their bounty would bring the sport to its knees.

The punters' present level of contribution is probably not too far removed from what is fair and reasonable, but it leaves the Levy Board to execute something approaching the wisdom of Solomon when it comes to distributing the cash it has available. Maintaining prize-money levels takes the largest slice of levy cake – nearly £11.5 million in 1982 – and here a balance has to be struck between the amounts allocated to the valuable prestigious races, where international comparisons are drawn, and the more humble run-of-the-mill contests which provide the broad base of the racing pyramid.

The élitist theory that the 'Pattern' and 'Listed' races – the showpieces of the industry – should be preserved against inflation, and whenever possible, increased in value to maintain or improve their position in the international league table, met with little approval from the grass roots of the sport when it was proposed that this could be achieved at the expense of the prize money allocated to more mundane contests. Not surprisingly, the advocates of such a policy were mainly those with extensive racing and breeding interests who dominate the upper echelons of the bloodstock markets, and whose concern for the viability of the small owner, trainer, jockey and racecourse company is not always apparent.

However, it would be equally wrong to devalue the prize money of the prestige races simply because of the rich rewards earned by the owner when the animal goes to stud. For the majority of owners, particularly those involved with steeplechasing and hurdling, there is little prospect of increasing the capital value of their horses and the modest prizes on the smaller courses are the most to which they can aspire. Here they can be lucky enough to win half a dozen races a year with a horse and still not cover their costs.

The conflicting interests of large and small owners render the Levy Board's task more difficult, particularly as it is unlikely that there will ever be sufficient money in the kitty to satisfy everyone.

Nor is it only prize money which the Levy Board is called upon to finance. There is scarcely a racecourse in the country which does not enjoy a new or modernized grandstand made possible by a grant or a loan from the Board. Starting stalls, camera patrol equipment, photo-finish equipment, stable security, dope testing, race commentaries, veterinary research, stable lads' hostels and canteens are all financed out of the Levy, requiring a touch of wizardry which Sir Ian Trethowan now undertakes to provide in succession to Lord Plummer, who retired after nine years as the highly adept chief financial juggler of the industry. But, of course, the Levy Board cannot function without the punter maintaining his interest in the sport. Indeed, the Chancellor of the Exchequer, too, would be hard hit without the turnover which keeps 12,000 betting shops in business. Phil Bull, whose *Timeform* provides the industry with its own invaluable bible, had a point when he commented on one occasion that it was everyone's patriotic duty to drink, smoke and bet as much as reasonably possible, or the country would be bankrupt!

TERRY WOGAN

IF YOU EVER GO ACROSS THE SEA
TO
CHELTENHAM

TO HORSE! TO HORSE!

Several years ago, in its infinite wisdom, the BBC saw fit to send me to the National Hunt Festival Meeting at Cheltenham, to present the afternoon's mix of racing and records, whimsy and waffle for Radio 2, the Manly Station.

'What,' they reasoned, with the sort of demented logic of which the Borgias and the BBC mandarins are made, 'could be more appropriate than to send an Irishman to cover the meeting which the Irish have regarded as their own ever since Niall of the Nine Hostages kidnapped St Patrick at a point-to-point meeting in North Wales?'

And so, with an icy wind ripping through my sheepskin and corrugated-iron underwear as though it were chiffon, I joined the invasion fleet, most of which seemed hellbent on making the British bookies pay for the Battle of the Boyne, drinking Gloucestershire out of Guinness, and reminding those English present that today was St Patrick's Day.

Threading my way through the shamrock-bedecked racegoers, it was not difficult to understand why Aer Lingus and the Irish ferries make a fortune in the middle of March each year. The vast natural amphitheatre of the racecourse must be one of the most dramatic settings for racing anywhere in the world. And guaranteed, every year, is the most superb steeplechasing and hurdle racing attracting the best of British and Irish horses to 18 races with prize money totalling more than £350,000.

Of course, there isn't an Irishman born (except, perhaps, me) who doesn't reckon that he is a better judge of a horse than the next man, provided that the next man is the worse for drink, so it is natural that he should put himself to the supreme test where it matters most; where national pride is every bit as much at stake as the Punts invested on it; where a winning Irish jockey is an immediate folk hero, and where training giants like Vincent O'Brien, Dan Moore, Tom Dreaper and Eddie O'Grady carved out their reputations in the rocky shadows of Cleeve Hill. And isn't it an Irish horse, the mighty Arkle, whose bronze statue dominates the magnificent new parade ring at the Mecca of jumping?

'Irish Punts Not Accepted' say the notices in the bars and on the bookmakers' boards, though judging by their customers they could just as well say 'Punts Not Pounds Taken' and adjust their prices accordingly. But no matter, the Allied Irish Bank is there to act as money-changer, though the story goes that when the bank opened its doors on the first day of the meeting a few years ago it started with £1½ million in sterling under the counter, but had run out before the first race.

Armed with the readies, the annual assault on the bookies begins. It is a point of honour among the men from Tipperary, Limerick or Wicklow never to take less than 9–2 about a 4–1 chance, and not for them is it a question of sticking on a pound or two, or even a fiver. The Irish National Debt must be repaid, and who better to do it for them than William Hill, Ladbroke's or the Tote.

CHELTENHAM

Nor, really, is it a gamble backing an Irish horse. Unless, perhaps, there is more than one in the race. At least, that's the way the Irish look at it. Right, and St Patrick, are on their side, and, just to make sure, most of the groups bring their parish priest with them. He, after all, has a hot line to where these things are decided.

Not that the priests themselves are novices when it comes to picking winners. It was Father Murphy himself, away over from Donegal, who was standing eyeing the horses in the parade ring at Cheltenham before the first race. Next to him was Rabbi Cohen, who watched in amazement as the holy father solemnly blessed one of the Irish challengers murmuring 'Dominus Vobiscum' as it walked past. The horse duly won, to the consternation of the Rabbi who had backed a tip given to him with the greatest confidence by little Hymie only that morning.

Before the next race, the two men again stood alongside each other. Again the horse blessed by Father Murphy won. Again the Rabbi's selection was beaten. And so it went on through the afternoon until the last race when the Rabbi could contain himself no longer. 'I've vatched you,' he said, 'all ze avternoon. You say "Dominus Vobiscum" and bless ze horse vitch vins. How can you do it?'

The Revd Murphy murmured something about the power of prayer and moved away leaving the Rabbi bewildered. But as Hymie's final choice approached he glanced furtively round, mumbled 'Dominus Vobiscum' and quickly made the Sign of the Cross over the horse. It got beaten.

'Vye,' he cried to Father Murphy as they met leaving the course, 'does zis mumbo jumbo not vork vor me?'

Ah, to be sure,' replied his reverence, 'it's just that you can't pick horses, and any fool could have told you not to try in an amateur riders' hunters' chase!'

The Irish do, of course, put a great deal into Cheltenham, even if their primary object is to take away the prize money and empty the bookmakers' satchels. Most of them pay handsomely at the gate for the best enclosures, though on the day of my BBC visit I heard of one who had sought to avoid this formality by climbing through the open window of a building on the perimeter of the course. It was the Police Office!

And Waterford Glass, famed for their crystal throughout the world, sponsor not only the Champion Hurdle itself but two other championship races on the opening day of the meeting. So confident are they of presenting the magnificent trophies to an Irish owner that they keep duplicates in Ireland to save shipping the huge suite of crystal back again across the Channel!

Another reason why Cheltenham is a spiritual home for

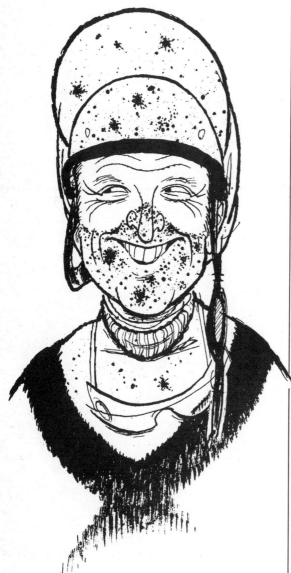

every Irish racegoer worthy of the name, is the weather. 'Clement' is not the word for it. On every occasion I have visited there, either professionally or socially, it's been tipping it down. Most of the time, Peter O'Sullevan seems more in need of a periscope than binoculars. And in my own experience there can be few less stimulating activities than doing a 'live' outside broadcast while the zephyrs are blowing sleet up your nose. . . .

My own day at Cheltenham ended as I tried to interview Jonjo O'Neill, the English-based, County Cork-bred jockey who had just ridden Alverton to win the Gold Cup. But I hadn't really appreciated the fervour of my fellow-countrymen, for although Alverton was English-owned and Yorkshire-trained, to be sure, wasn't he *ridden* by an Irishman, and on St Patrick's Day too! There we were in the unsaddling enclosure discussing the finer points of horsemanship when an over-enthusiastic and over-Guinnessed supporter jumped the rails, rushed up to Jonjo, threw his arms round his neck and screamed: 'Jonjo, you're a whore, a terrible whore.'

Where he came from, it was pronounced 'hooer', and in certain circumstances, such as obtained at the present time, it was a high compliment, meaning a 'shrewd rogue', or a 'clever rascal'. He didn't care what it meant to ten million listeners to Radio 2 through my 'live' mike. To him Jonjo was a hero – and that's just what he said! Funny thing was, I didn't get one letter of complaint. Maybe no-one was listening . . . as usual.

NEWMARKET

TO HORSE! TO HORSE!

Newmarket is by no means the oldest racecourse in Britain – and in comparison to the Roodeye at Chester, where the Romans enjoyed their racing under Ben Hur rules two thousand years ago, it is still a fledgling. Just what King James I was doing on the Cambridgeshire/ Suffolk borders on 27 February 1605, history does not relate. Certainly, Newmarket in February is no place to go in search of a winter sunshine break. But that was the date on which he first saw the rolling acres of heathland, a sporting paradise which was rapidly to become his favourite hunting ground.

One thing led to another, and 17 years later the first recorded horse race took place on the wide open spaces which have since become the most famous racing centre in the world. James's son, Charles I, got into all sorts of bother before Oliver Cromwell finally chopped his head off, so he had little opportunity for racing against anything but time as he tried to keep one jump ahead of the Roundheads.

However, when the monarchy was restored in 1660 Charles II had no such preoccupation, and like his grandfather he found in Newmarket the ideal playground to which he could take his court, Nell Gwyn, a basket of oranges and a string of racehorses.

Charles rode in many of the races himself, and founded the Newmarket Town Plate, a race which is still run today and which in 1981 made its own little bit of history by becoming the first race in modern times to take place in England on a Sunday. Charles also became the ultimate racing authority of his day, adjudicating in the disputes which were inevitable as the sport grew in stature and popularity.

Although the 'Sport of Kings' was firmly established by the time Charles II died in 1685, his immediate successors showed little interest in racing, apart from Queen Anne who had a number of horses trained at Newmarket, and, more importantly, founded Ascot Racecourse.

But racing itself thrived, and courses sprang up like mushrooms to rival Newmarket which, lacking Royal patronage, entered a lean spell. However, in about 1750 the more influential supporters of racing, the embryo Jockey Club, moved their base of operations from London to Newmarket, and racing, not to mention a host of less desirable pursuits, gave back to the town the sort of prominence it had enjoyed a hundred years earlier. Indeed, cock fighting, bear baiting and the more exclusive brothels which opened up branch offices in the town made Newmarket a Mecca for the Regency rakes. Gambling was uncontrolled, vast fortunes were won and lost, and no-one seemed too fussy about what they bet on. One particularly revolting individual actually made a huge wager on his ability to eat a live cat; he later showed some small spark of decency by committing suicide.

Racing in the mid-18th century was

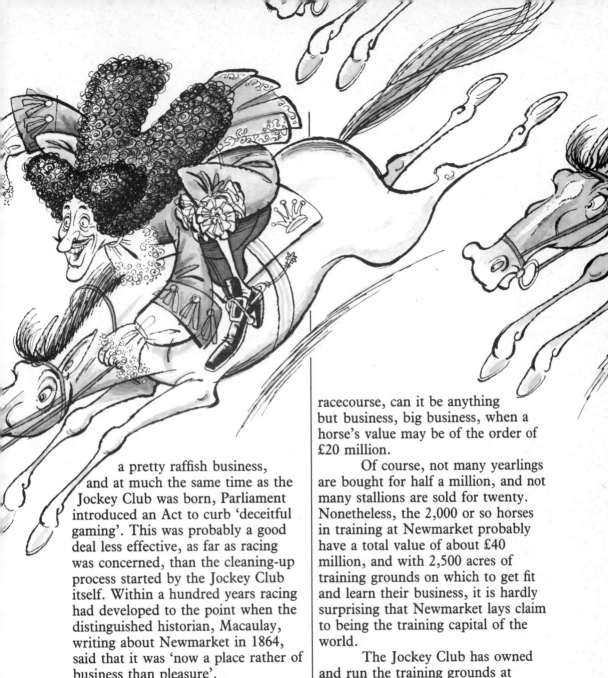

a pretty raffish business, and at much the same time as the Jockey Club was born, Parliament introduced an Act to curb 'deceitful gaming'. This was probably a good deal less effective, as far as racing was concerned, than the cleaning-up process started by the Jockey Club itself. Within a hundred years racing had developed to the point when the distinguished historian, Macaulay, writing about Newmarket in 1864, said that it was 'now a place rather of business than pleasure'.

Today it is very much a place of business. Yearlings costing upwards of half a million pounds cannot be given less than the highest standards of professional training. Nor, if they should become part of that tiny élite selected for the most prestigious stallion duties as a result of a spectacular career on the racecourse, can it be anything but business, big business, when a horse's value may be of the order of £20 million.

Of course, not many yearlings are bought for half a million, and not many stallions are sold for twenty. Nonetheless, the 2,000 or so horses in training at Newmarket probably have a total value of about £40 million, and with 2,500 acres of training grounds on which to get fit and learn their business, it is hardly surprising that Newmarket lays claim to being the training capital of the world.

The Jockey Club has owned and run the training grounds at Newmarket for the best part of two hundred years, although recently the ownership was vested technically in a more prosaic-sounding property company. So meticulously are the training gallops controlled that the strips – up to 28 miles of them – are marked out for use on two or three days together and then may not be used again for up to three years. And with 1,700 acres of gallops available on the Heath, good fresh ground is always available for use by the forty-odd trainers.

But Newmarket is not just a town devoted to training thoroughbred horses. Many magnificent and historic stud farms also make it the breeding centre of Britain. The National Stud – one of the most profitable concerns in the 'Public Sector' – rivals any similar establishment in the world. The Derby winners Mill Reef, Grundy, Royal Palace and Blakeney are among the National Stud's nine stallions; five of them are resident at Newmarket, and each annually enjoys the favours of about forty mares whose owners pay up to £30,000 for the privilege.

Tattersalls Sales Ring and Paddocks dominate the south side of the town, and prices paid there for foals, yearlings and older horses can be mind-boggling. There are veterinary practices, saddlers, colour makers, farriers, bloodstock agents, bookmakers, horse transport companies, and feed merchants. But just to prove that everything on four legs in Newmarket is not a racehorse, the Pork Shop sells as fine a sausage as you will buy anywhere!

The Equine Research Station provides not only a horse hospital as impressive as any in the world but, as its name implies, a veterinary research centre whose contribution to racing on five continents has been invaluable. The laboratories of Racecourse Security Services are also housed at Newmarket: the vigilance of their scientists and the strict rules of the Jockey Club have combined in the virtual elimination of criminal doping.

Then there are the two racecourses at Newmarket, both of which provide a consistently high standard of racing. The Rowley Mile, named after Charles II (Old Rowley himself), is broader than any course in the world, with an undulating straight mile and a quarter stretching out to the horizon. Its grandstands, four-square, solid grey, formidable and spacious, offer some refuge from the spring and autumn winds which can rip through Newmarket. Nonetheless, thousands of racegoers would readily face even more chilling conditions to see the first two Classic races of the season, the 1,000 and 2,000 Guineas, or the big autumn handicaps, the Cambridgeshire and the Cesarewitch.

For the summer months there is the more intimate, informal and colourful July Course, where the buildings are thatched, the bars half hidden in woodland glades and the trees give shelter from the unrelenting sun – on the day that it shines. Like Royal Ascot, but without the formality, the July Meeting combines a garden-party atmosphere with top-class racing.

But Newmarket, for all its professionalism, its racecourses, its studs, its stables, sale rings and laboratories is still a little country town. And it hasn't changed that much since King James first saw it in 1605, or King Charles held court on Warren Hill. Newmarket to them meant the vast expanse of rolling heath, and that is really what Newmarket is all about today.

TERRY WOGAN
ROYAL ASCOT

TO HORSE! TO HORSE!

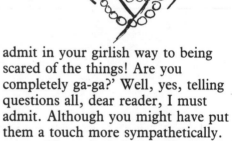

Elsewhere in this noble tome, you will find reference to Wogan, T, as the bookie's friend, the man who makes sure that Joe Coral wants for nothing, whose foolproof system of never knowingly backing a winner helps to keep Mrs Ladbroke and all her brood in the comfort to which they have become accustomed. You will hear tell of the abuse heaped on my cowering head by justifiably incensed punters, of how Julian Wilson looks down his nose at me, and Lord Oaksey hides behind his hat at the mention of my name. Even jockeys look down on me.

'Why, then,' I hear you cry, 'why then, you dumb plutz, do you go racing at all? Why leave your dingy little studio and expose yourself to all this gratuitous abuse? You know nothing about horses, you

admit in your girlish way to being scared of the things! Are you completely ga-ga?' Well, yes, telling questions all, dear reader, I must admit. Although you might have put them a touch more sympathetically.

If you must know, I'm a *social* racing man, that's why. A gay, madcap creature, a flibbertigibbet. Pleasure-bent, and living for the moment. For me, the pop of the champagne cork, the tinkle of fine crystal, the whiff of the Monte Cristo is all. And for the likes of me, there is only one outing, only one race meeting truly worthy of the name. Shout it from your crenellated castle ramparts! Mention it with pride! Ascot! Royal Ascot! Morning suits and toppers! Good old Moss Bros! Smoked salmon and champoo! Roly-Polys as far as the eye can see! Nothing less than a Turbo-Porsche in the car park!

Horses? Who said anything about *horses*? Tho' I'm told that for those who like 'em, there is no better four days' racing in the calendar. But for most of us, Royal Ascot's the place to be *seen*! Fifty thousand people in search of Nigel Dempster. Or, failing him, Lady Olga Maitland, William Hickey or Jennifer. Even that ghastly fella on *Private Eye* will do, at a push. Thursday's the Big One: Ladies' Day. Look! There's Mrs Shilling, somewhere under one of her son's hats. Oh, no, it's only a marquee . . . . See how the 'models' strain, like greyhounds in the slips, for the eye of the camera. 'Great Heavens, Daphne! Are you wearing that frock for a bet?!'

Self-styled 'Seducers of the Valleys' and 'Debs' Delights' vie eagerly for Nigel's ear. How else will anyone know they're there? How else will *they* know? Who's *In*? Who's

Out? 'Are you sure you didn't wear that hat *last* year, darling?' You can't hear yourself think for the whinnying – and it's not all coming from the stables . . . .

It's extraordinary, but as Britain's fortunes have unfortunately declined, so Royal Ascot, with its ostentatious display, its conspicuous consumption, seems to have become more popular. In the past couple of years, in the trough of the worst depression this country has seen for fifty years, the crowds have been greater, the limousines glossier, the clothes more expensive, the bets bigger than ever. Yes, I *do* go. *And* I love it. If you can't cock a snook at life occasionally, and fling a custard pie in the face of ill-fortune, then they really *have* ground you down.

We're lucky enough to have good friends who invite us to their box on Ladies' Day, and it's one of

TO HORSE! TO HORSE!

the highlights of our year. It's a day full of food, drink, laughter and song. The song is usually *The Queen of Connemara* or *They're Cutting the Corn Around Creslough Today*, for the singer is a sweet-voiced tenor from the West of Ireland. What the denizens of the adjoining boxes make of these Irish Ballads on a very English occasion, I can't imagine, but they join in the choruses all right.

We never mind the milling throng that keeps us from the Royal Enclosure, the traffic jams that make us too late to see the Royal Procession down the course, and, usually, too late for the first race. Who cares if you never get a bet on all day, not to mind see a horse? It's being there, among friends, that counts. Anyway, I'm convinced that most of the people are only there to watch other people.

The other year, the person they most wanted to see was that Ol' Houn' Dawg from Texas, the Rat-Bag hisself – J R Ewing! Larry Hagman, a sucker for punishment if ever I saw one, attended Royal Ascot every day, signed joke dollar bills and loved every minute of the hustle, bustle and tradition of it all. He plunged in and out of the heaving mass of millinery with his stetson in one hand and his grey topper in the other yelling 'Howdy y'all!' to all and sundry.

Jest another cotton-pickin' social Racin'-man, I guess.

TO HORSE! TO HORSE!

It is inconceivable that anyone designing a racecourse which would be regarded throughout the world as the supreme test for three year-olds racing over a mile and a half would come up with anything remotely resembling the Derby course at Epsom. Indeed, Epsom was never designed. It just happened – a racecourse staked out on the Downs above a fashionable spa town to provide further recreation for the Londoners who flocked there in the 18th century to take the waters and pass the time in the more bloodthirsty pursuits of cock fighting and the prize ring. One can even imagine that those who stuck the first marker-posts into the downland turf would have been worried about the suitability of the terrain with its testing climbs and steep descent, yet in making the best of the land available to them they were to create a course which would attract visitors from the farthest corners of the world every summer to witness a race which Disraeli was later to dub the Blue Ribbon of the Turf.

The Derby itself was first run in 1780 as a complementary race to the Oaks which was inaugurated in the previous year. Devised by the 12th Earl of Derby and his house-party guests, who included the then Senior Steward of the Jockey Club, Sir Charles Bunbury, the new race reflected the changes taking place in racing: greater emphasis was now given to three year-olds competing over shorter distances than the four miles or so over which older horses were more commonly tested.

The Oaks, named after Lord Derby's Epsom villa, proved a great success, but was confined then, as it is now, to fillies. The new race was to be for colts and fillies. Its title was decided on the toss of a coin, between the host and his guest of honour, and while Sir Charles Bunbury lost that particular contest he was to gain rapid consolation when his horse Diomed won the first Derby. Sir Charles was to win his second Derby 21 years later with Eleanor, one of only six fillies to have won the premier classic in its 203-

year history.

Lord Derby was to win the race himself in 1787 with Sir Peter Teazle, but thereafter his family had to wait 137 years before they won their race again, with Sansovino. Nine years later the Derby colours were carried by Hyperion to record their third success, and a fourth came in the 1942 wartime Derby run at Newmarket.

The Derby course, run over a mile for the first four years of its history, has altered little since it was extended to a mile and a half in 1784, and has been virtually unchanged since 1872. What makes it truly unique among racecourses is the rise and fall of the ground between the start and finish. From the time the horses leave the stalls to the moment they reach the top of the hill at the halfway point, they will have climbed 134 feet. After levelling off for 300 yards they turn left-handed as the course begins the steep descent to Tattenham Corner. Here there is a drop of 40 feet in 330 yards, and as the horses turn into the finishing straight it appears from the stands that they race on the level before starting to climb again in the last quarter of a mile. In fact this is an optical illusion, for after rounding Tattenham Corner the horses continue downhill and descend a further 56 feet until they reach a point about 100 yards from the winning-post, after which they climb three feet to the finish. To complicate matters still further, there is a natural camber in the finishing straight, and a six-foot drop between the stand and the inside rails on the finishing line.

No-one could plan a course

like this, but the result of such a happy accident is the supreme test calling for stamina, balance, adaptability and rapid acceleration. Indeed, it is no accident that the Derby is never won by a poor horse although, of course, some winners are inevitably better than others. Nor is it a coincidence that a horse which negotiates the twists and turns, the gradients and the cambers better than his opponents is immediately one of the hottest stallion prospects in the world with a value running into many millions.

But while the racing world and the pundits are assessing the quality and the value of the combatants, the public who flock to Epsom on Derby Day are more likely to concern themselves with less weighty matters. For two hundred years or more Derby Day has had an atmosphere all its own. Fortune-tellers, swings, roundabouts and sideshows provide all the fun of the fair for a crowd estimated at between a quarter and half a million, the vast majority of whom remain on common land outside the racecourse enclosures and therefore pay nothing to witness the world's greatest horserace. Open-topped buses have

replaced the horse-drawn carriages of a bygone age, seedy strip shows the cock-fighting pits, and an unattractive race of mobile-home dwellers the traditional Romany Gypsies of old. But the card-sharpers and petty villains who will quickly separate the unwary fool from his money are as evident today as they were a hundred years ago.

No longer, however, is the Downs bookmaker likely to make the Derby winner look like a tortoise by fleeing his pitch before pay-out time. Nor does Parliament any longer shut up shop to allow Lords and Commoners alike to join the general exodus from London to the hurly burly of Epsom Downs. But the picnics remain – iced champagne, gulls' eggs and game pie from Fortnum's spread out behind the Rolls Royce parked alongside a pickup whose passengers are equally content with warm brown ale, jellied eels and a leg of Kentucky Fried Chicken. The chances are that the parties will intermingle happily as rumour and counter-rumour spread about the well-being of the big-race favourite, or the state of the Kingston Bypass for the journey home.

Before the start of racing all eyes will be on the course as Her Majesty the Queen is driven slowly down the straight to the cheers of thousands of throats. Alighting at the finishing-post, she stands amid a curious stillness while the National Anthem is played, and takes her place in the Royal Box as the hubbub of Derby Day again reaches a crescendo. A

couple of hours later the race is run. The fortunate owner is several million pounds richer, the bookmakers will count their losses or stash their profits. The punters will celebrate or console themselves with another bottle or two, and the winning horse will be loaded into his box without really knowing what all the fuss was about. The big dipper and the dodgems will provoke screams of excitement in the fairground, Gypsy Rose Lee will peer into her crystal ball, which somehow was not tuned into the right form book before racing began, but which now reveals all for a oncer, and the fish-and-chip stalls will be wrapping their wares in now-discarded copies of *The Sporting Life*. The strippers will reveal their G-strings for the umpteenth time of the day, and half a dozen happy streakers will race along the last fifty yards of the Derby course pursued by as many weary policemen. Derby Day is over for another year. It was much the same two hundred years ago, and like as not it will be much the same in two hundred years from now.

TERRY WOGAN

LA VIE PARISIENNE, OR, SUIVEZ CE CHEVAL!

TO HORSE! TO HORSE!

The French being so very, well, French, have a word for it: *Le Racing*. They *would*, wouldn't they? Can't think up one of their own, so they nick the Word according to Newmarket.

I wouldn't mind if *Le Racing* bore any smidgin of resemblance to the *real* thing, as endured by the hardy British racegoer. Where, I ask you, is the similarity between Carlisle in January and Cagnes-sur-Mer in May? Point out, if you will, any approximation of Towcester or Fakenham to Chantilly or Longchamp. There are, I'll grant you, certain superficial similarities to delude the naive, or naif. Horses for instance. Jockeys, too. The odd pair of binoculars. But where are the battered brown hats? The soup-stained off-green raincoats? The tweed suits with the half-mast trousers and turn-ups? The brogue shoes? The shooting sticks? The bookies? Aha!

Mark you, *Les Français* attempt to ape their betters in tartans from The Scotch House or the odd Irish Walking Hat from Dunn's, but it doesn't come anywhere close, *mes braves*. It's too pat, too neat by half. They don't *even* have Brown Windsor soup in the restaurants, nor, if you can believe it, that stout bulwark of all that's best in British racing: the Steak and Kidney Pie!

How, then, is the racegoer possibly expected to give of his best on a diet of *crudités, grenouilles, filet de barbue à l'estragon* and *petit pot au chocolat*? Mind you, by the time he's paid for all that at Longchamp, he'd have nothing left to give, anyway.

LA VIE PARISIENNE

In case you think this is all second-hand stuff, let me tell you (droned the ageing boulevardier) that I've been to Longchamp more than once. Twice, actually. I flew in to Le Bourget on a wing and a prayer from Gatwick, with my Senior Racing Advisor and fellow-scribe, the sainted Fairbairn, along with members of the Racegoers' Club. All of us eager to savour the delights of Paris and take the French Tote to the cleaners.

First of all, we took a pre-racing luncheon swing at Le Paris des Gourmets. A very nice chop it was too, with *petits pois* straight from the tin, followed by a *crème caramel* that would have been distinguished in any motorway café. Having battered our way around the Boulevard Périphérique several times, we eventually found the correct *Porte*, and then joined the millimetre-by-millimetre crawl through the Bois de Boulogne to the racetrack at Longchamp.

Longchamp itself is a fair treat: the grandstand, a triumph of modern racecourse design, with a peerless view of the course, and beyond, across the tree-tops, the spike of the Eiffel Tower. The *ambience* is *très agréable, aussi*. Chic abounds. It is the merest of steps from the grandstand to the parade ring. On every *coin* there seems to be a closed-circuit colour-television monitor, giving the pampered racegoer the latest prices, and sovereign views of the ring, the paddock and the racecourse. It's *le dernier cri*, and a far cry from the public-school spartan surroundings of most British race-tracks. Even Ascot itself could learn from Longchamp.

Indeed, those who attend this Versailles of racing have only one, teensy-weensy criticism of it. It doesn't work, on two rather trivial levels: 1) You can't get a bet *on*, and 2) You can't get a drink *in*.

The honest turf accountant is *de trop* in France, and the frustrated punter has but one target at which to hurl his hard-earned *chemise*: the *Pari Mutuel*. Unfortunately, at Longchamp *Le Mutuel* can't cope. If you want to bet on the third race, you'd better start queueing before the end of the first. If you are not familiar with French racecourse *patois*, then you'd be better off joining the thirsty at the bar. In fact, depending of course on your racing priorities, you'd be *far* better off taking station at the bar, and *before* racing starts. On the two occasions on which I attended for Le Prix de l'Arc de Triomphe the bars at Longchamp ran out of *everything*, including Perrier water, long before the *fin*.

The French, at the risk of botching the *Entente Cordiale*, haven't really mastered *Le Racing*. And don't bother mentioning the names of Boussac, Head, Boutin, or yet Yves Saint-Martin. Most people think the last-named makes frocks anyway, and it will only confuse the issue. *Non, mes petits*, the trouble with our cross-Channel chums is that they think *Le Racing* is a *social* occasion. It's just an excuse for an endless lunch and interminable conversation. In this, the French resemble their Celtic cousins, the Irish, if you substitute 'liquid' for 'lunch'. The difference with the Irish, of course, is that, along with the drinking and talking,

they're also hurling lumps of money at the bookies. Any Irish racecourse that did not relieve the punter of his 'punts' quicker than he could dip his hand into his hempen trews, would be sunk in the Bog of Allen before the end of the first day's racing. The French give one the saddening impression that they couldn't care less if they *never* stuck a *sou sur le nez*. They lack *l'esprit*, if not *de corps*, then *du cheval*. Too thrifty by half.

Anyway, who the Sam Hill wants to go racing when he can play the gay blade, the *insouçiant* boulevardier along the Champs Elysées or in Pigalle? Queuing for the privilege of putting a bet on cannot possible hold a candle to sipping a cognac and watching *le tout Paris* meander by along the Boulevard St Germain. No, my littles, it's all too distracting. The hardy British punter is much more at home enduring the privations of Carlisle, or Folkestone, where the chic-est thing you'll see is the Duke of Devonshire's hat, or Henry Cecil's trousers . . . .

TONY FAIRBAIRN
RACING ROUND
THE
WORLD

TO HORSE! TO HORSE!

Foreigners, as every English schoolboy knows, begin at Calais, and by and large their abilities are limited to the production of funny food, naughty women and rather excitable footballers. Some of the more acceptable ones (foreigners, not women) play rugby and cricket, thanks to the civilizing influences of our ancestors, but otherwise their sporting attainments seem restricted to professional rounders, sticking spears into rump steak on the hoof, and screaming abuse at tennis umpires. They do, however, have one thing in common. They're not British. (This applies also to the Irish, but that is quite another story, and because they live very close by, and almost speak English, they enjoy a special category of their own.)

Foreigners can and do have some endearing characteristics, not least of which is to enjoy their horse racing in the sort of comfort which us Brits regard as cissy, and to finance such luxury out of the profits of Tote Monopoly Betting. This is un-British, unsporting and unfair. Not only can foreigners never profit from the character-building qualities of an afternoon's racing in the pouring rain or an icy wind, refreshed by warm beer and an English sandwich, but if they lose they cannot even console themselves with the thought that they are keeping some poor bookmaker in Krug and caviar. Selfishly, they can anticipate only the thicker carpets, warmer radiators and plushier seats which the management will instal out of the betting profits.

With so many packaged tours available to The Abroad, more and more holidaymakers now leave Britain each year to enjoy not only sunshine and sub-tropical beaches, but to see for themselves the sybaritic existence of the foreign racegoer. And make no mistake about it, racing abroad can be great fun, even if it's not quite as exciting as Wolverhampton on a wet Monday in February. You must not be put off by having to sit in a grandsit rather than stand in a grandstand, or by the fact that foreigners wouldn't dream of constructing a racecourse at which the spectators couldn't see all the way round. The fact that it is relatively cheap to go racing abroad should not deter the intrepid traveller, and it is not difficult to remove the ice discreetly from a gin and tonic or walk up a staircase instead of using one of the many escalators. Small sacrifices have to be made.

Having accepted this, the Brit will find racing in America, Australia, the Orient, Africa, or closer home in Europe much the same as at his local course. Once through the turnstiles, his fellow racegoers will be huddled in little groups discussing the form of races past and the prospects of races to come. Furrowed faces will study the pages of the *Derby News* in Tokyo with the same intensity as the American will scan the *Daily Racing Form*, the Frenchman *Paris Turf*, or the Englishman his *Sporting Life* or *Chronicle*. In most countries – but not, strangely, America – the horses will come under close scrutiny in the parade ring, and the jubilation of a winning punter is much the same the world over. Crowds can become a little more animated with funny Frenchmen screaming 'Voleur, voleur' at any jockey who appears to have ridden an injudicious race, or South American arsonists setting light to the Stewards' Room after an unpopular decision. Americans tend to shout 'Aw, shit' when a favourite gets stuffed, Australians something similar between gulps of Fosters, while the Japanese shake their heads sadly from side to side as they go in search of a hot towel and a cup of green tea. Chinese, however, chatter like starlings at roost after every race, and Germans scowl grimly at the judge and anyone else who might have caused their downfall.

Most British racegoers seeking to broaden their experience of The Abroad start with France. This is a mistake. To begin with the French don't speak English, and don't see why they should. Consequently there are communication problems, and even the most experienced punter betting twice a week on the Tote at Walthamstow dogs can get into difficulties with *gagne* and *place*, not to mention *jambon*, and *omelette fromage*, *pommes frites* and *petits pois*. Like far too many other countries the French also operate in metres rather than furlongs. But simply divide by two and knock off the noughts, for 1,600 metres is eight furlongs or one mile. Their weights, though, are in kilos, which are complicated. At Longchamp, the Mecca of French racing, the commentaries are largely unintelligible except to the French, although the cunning racegoer can listen for one phrase which will tell him what's what in all middle- and long-distance races. 'Apres le petit

bois' is used in every commentary; it has nothing to do with green peas, but indicates the order of the horses as they emerge from behind a clump of trees a mile or so from the finish.

To confuse matters further, the French insist upon frenchifying perfectly good English names, and several thousand Brits were totally mystified a few years ago by reference to a horse called Ig-est-op-eeze, when they had staked their all on Highest Hopes.

Longchamp is very beautiful, but wining and dining there is very expensive. A winner should be celebrated with the purchase of a small *bière* and several glasses rather than the most modest champagne which costs roughly the same as a stallion nomination to the winner of their great race, the Prix de l'Arc de Triomphe. The *Grande Piste*, the *Moyenne Piste* and the *Petite Piste* refer therefore not to states of inebriation but to three different tracks at the course. On Arc Day, Longchamp is chaotic with ten thousand Brits falling about trying to see the horses, have a drink, make a bet and watch each race, an impossibility which the experienced compromise over by betting in England before they leave, and remaining in the bar to watch the sport on television.

Another French racecourse which is a popular target for British racegoers is the charming little *piste* – and many of them are – at Cagnes-sur-Mer, strategically placed between Cannes and Nice on the Côte d'Azur. This is much more like home, a sort of small Goodwood with garlic, where the racing is a combination of flat and jumping with a dose of the trots thrown in. The trots, it must be explained, refer in this case to trotting races where enormous men sit in little buggies pulled by medium-sized horses who are prevented by the driver from going as fast as they can.

Crossing the Alps into Italy can provide racegoers with good sport too. The Italians have more conferences about racing than the United Nations do about nuclear disarmament, so they and their visitors become totally confused. They tend towards a Tote Monopoly, but contrarily licence a few bookmakers. However, as most Italians seem to prefer to bet with the unlicensed bookmakers who operate quite openly, they seem to settle for the worst of all worlds. The racecourses are attractive, the racegoers excitable and sums of money have so many noughts on the end that the most modest win makes punters feel like millionaires.

German racing is, as you would expect, highly efficient. Unfortunately they ensure that many of their big prizes are won by German horses simply by refusing to accept entries from other countries. Baden-Baden is the place to go. Norway, too, is well worth a visit, and the racecourse at Ovrevoll outside Oslo can be great fun. The British are always made most welcome, and unlike the Germans they like to see English horses running on their courses. The Racegoers' Club visited Norway a few years ago, and so keen were the Norwegians that the Club bring one of its horses that they framed a race

in such a way that the £4,000 prize could only be won by the English horse. It seemed like taking candy from a baby. Unfortunately Concession Day, the filly concerned, didn't much care for the fjords, vikings and smorgesbord, ate her bed of straw the night before the race and trotted home a well-beaten fifth.

Across the Atlantic, Kentucky is now better known for its multi-million dollar wall-to-wall stallion syndicates than fried chicken. Thoroughbred breeding in the States has, however, learned something from Colonel Sanders, for while mares and foals are not yet kept in batteries, production-line techniques have taken much of the romance out of procreation, and the few brief seconds allowed for mating mean that equine small talk on such occasions is virtually non-existent.

But if horse breeding owes something to factory farming, it's nothing compared to the racecourses. They are highly mechanized, highly efficient money factories, animated betting shops referred to by their managements as 'The Plant'. Aqueduct, the Big A, outside New York has its own railway station, and with racing taking place daily for several months at a time, attracts big enough crowds each afternoon to justify it. Everything revolves around 'the handle', the money staked each day, and upon which the racecourse is largely dependent for its revenue. This applies to every racecourse in the States, but while Aqueduct is rather soulless, many of their other courses have great character and charm. Aqueduct's sister course, Belmont Park, is one such, while the

Californian tracks at Santa Anita, Hollywood Park, Golden Gate Fields and Bay Meadows are all very attractive. So, too, are the Florida courses, Hialeah, Gulfstream – founded by Jimmy Donn, a Scottish gardener from Lanark and now run by his grandson – and the newly opened Calder Park.

Unfortunately, from the British point of view, America is dominated by dirt racing, and somehow the sight of a great champion returning to the unsaddling enclosure covered in wet grey sand with the jockey's colours obliterated by the same mucky substance can never match up to the legendary pictures we have of Kelso, Swaps and Secretariat. The American courses do have grass tracks as well but they are used sparingly – as they have to be with each course racing daily for months on end. The system is highly efficient and the Americans can never understand the British moving from course to course every couple of days. Their rewards, however, lie in the facilities given to racegoers – everything except a bookmaker.

The Australian is a born gambler, and racing in the land of the Roo, Fosters Lager and Kerry Packer is a national institution. The courses are very English in character, as well they might be considering who founded most of them, and while they have a Tote Monopoly off-course, they do battle with some pretty fearless and intrepid bookmakers on the track. Their turnover per capita makes the British appear totally dominated by Gamblers Anonymous, and woe betide any jockey who makes a

nonsense of it when the chips are down. The big courses in Melbourne and Sydney compare favourably with any in the world, while many of the little country courses have great charm and atmosphere.

In South Africa, too, the English influence and tradition are strong, and the magnificent climate lends itself to sunny afternoons on lush green turf surrounded by exotic flowers. Capetown, Johannesburg and Durban have magnificent courses, well run and supplied by a thriving breeding industry. Betting takes place both on the Tote and with bookmakers.

Finally there is the Orient, probably the most extraordinary racing scene of all. The Chinese and the Japanese make even the Australians look like novices when it comes to betting, and they flock to their racecourses as though their lives depended upon it. Japanese racecourse managements drop their inscrutability to look almost disappointed if 100,000 or more fail to turn out every Saturday and Sunday for a marathon of racing which starts at ten o'clock in the morning and goes on with a break for lunch well into the afternoon. A dozen or so races with millions of yen invested on each ensures that Japan runs the most profitable racing in the world. There's off-course betting, too, and while there are restrictions on the number of betting shops there's no limit on their size, so the largest of the Tokyo shops occupies roughly the same space as Selfridges in London's Oxford Street, and like Selfridges it trades on five floors. This one shop has its own railway station and expects about 80,000 customers a day.

The racing itself is expertly organized – though what British jockeys would say about being locked away from their wives, and everyone else's wives, the night before racing, is open to speculation. Less happily, and despite all the money available, Japanese breeders will never hold their own in competition with horses bred in Europe and America. They can, and have, bought fine stallions, high-quality mares, and all the expertise available in the world. But their grassland pastures simply do not enjoy the right mixture of mineral content, and two generations are enough to turn the finest breeding lines into very moderate performers.

Hong Kong has no such problems. All horses are imported and quality is not of any great importance to them. Competitive racing is what the Royal Hong Kong Jockey Club seeks to provide and this it does twice a week to such good effect that admission to its two courses is by ticket only, purchased in advance. The racecourse at Happy Valley has been in existence for 140 years, and in the Seventies it was decided to expand the thriving racing programme and build a new course. Unfortunately in Hong Kong space is at a premium and the only solution was to site the new course on top of a mountain. Mountains, though, don't make good racecourses, so before the turf could be laid and the grandstands erected, the mountain had to be moved to sea level. So, lorry-load by lorry-load, the mountain top was transferred to fill an inlet from the sea and upon it was built Sha Tin – probably the finest racecourse in the world today. It is an unbelievable story, but such is the Chinese love of a gamble that the vast cost involved was recovered within a couple of years through the equally unbelievable betting turnover generated.

Singapore, too, has a thriving racing industry, and while it lacks the frenetic betting of Hong Kong and the magnificent opulence of Sha Tin, its Bukit Timah racecourse must lay claim to be one of the most beautiful in the world. Here too the horses are not world-beaters, but there's great sport to be had.

And that, whether it be in

RACING ROUND THE WORLD

America, Australia, Africa, Asia, the continent of Europe or Bangor-on-Dee, is what racing is all about. Oh, yes, it's about bloodlines and Classic races, it's about sporting owners, shrewd trainers, talented jockeys and devoted stable staff. It's about big business, Tote turnover, bookmakers' profitability and attendance figures. It's about brave horses and slow horses, fast horses and Wogan's Winners, it's about Turf pundits and TV commentators. But in essence it's about entertainment. It's a great sport, and great fun. Enjoy it.

TONY FAIRBAIRN

ACKNOWLEDGMENTS

Four long-suffering sons demand acknowledgment, not for any contribution to the book itself, but for their constant struggle to find a clean shirt while their mother typed the manuscript. To her I am extremely grateful; to any Chinese laundry proprietor I commend their new-found expertise. For expertise of a different kind my thanks are due to John Biggs of the Racehorse Owners Association; Colonel John Cameron-Hayes of the Racecourse Association; Louise Gold of the Racing Information Bureau; Tristram Ricketts, Secretary of the Horserace Betting Levy Board, and my friends at the Timeform Organization, in particular Reg Griffin and Graham Dench who supplied vital statistics, checked others, and generally tried to ensure that we have maintained a higher striking rate of accuracy here than in the daily prediction of Wogan's Winner.